A PERSONAL JOURNAL

WITH MEDITATIONS FROM

"GOD'S DREAM TEAM"

ANSWERING GOD'S PRAYER

"I PRAY...THAT THEY MAY BE ONE"—JESUS

TOMMY TENNEY

AUTHOR OF "THE GOD CHASERS"

Regal
FROM GOSPEL LIGHT

Published by Regal Books
A Division of Gospel Light
Ventura, California, U.S.A.
Printed in U.S.A.

Cover Design by Kevin Keller
Interior Design by Robert Williams
Edited by Larry Walker and David Webb

LIBRARY OF CONGRESS CATALOGING-IN-PUBLICATION DATA

Tenney, Tommy, 1956–
    Answering God's prayer / Tommy Tenney
        p. cm
    Includes bibliographical references
    ISBN 0-8307-2578-4 (pbk.)
    1. Church—Unity—Meditations.   2. Concord—Meditations   I Title

BV601.5 .T44   2000
262'.72—dc21   00-029677

2   3   4   5   6   7   8   9   10   11   12   13   14   15 / 09   08   07   06   05   04   03   02   01   00

Rights for publishing this book in other languages are contracted by Gospel Literature International (GLINT). GLINT also provides technical help for the adaptation, translation and publishing of Bible study resources and books in scores of languages worldwide. For further information, contact GLINT, P.O. Box 4060, Ontario, CA 91761-1003, U.S.A. You may also send e-mail to Glintint@aol.com, or visit their website at www.glint.org

CONTENTS

THOUGHTS FROM A MEMBER OF GOD'S DREAM TEAM

The journey to unity is just that—a journey taken one step at a time. As with most journeys into unknown or unfamiliar territory, the journey to unity requires a road map of sorts. If you have read my book *God's Dream Team*, then you know the biblical roots of God's only unanswered prayer can be traced back to the high-priestly prayer of Jesus in the Upper Room. Only hours before He gave up His life to purchase our freedom, Jesus prayed in passionate anguish, "Holy Father, keep through Your name those whom You have given Me, *that they may be one* as We are."[1]

This is God's dream for what is ordained to become His Dream Team, the Church. The practical outworking of God's dream is for all of His sons and daughters in any given church or city to flow together in the river of His presence and love in perfect *unity* as one Body.

The path to such unity is best described as a journey of steps by many to a single goal of eternal importance and value. The most important question for each of us is this: *What am I willing to do to answer God's prayer?*

Perhaps the first step is for us to learn how God defines unity so that we are better equipped to answer His prayer.

God's prayer is not only for us to be blessed individually, but to be blessed as a family by friends and friendships. Friendship is so important to God that He allowed Himself to be called a friend and He became our "friend who sticks closer than a brother."[2] He upgraded our status from servants, even when we didn't deserve it. Jesus said, "No longer do I call you servants, for a servant does not know what his master is doing; but I have called you friends, for all things that I heard from My Father I have made known to you."[3]

The problem with unity is that it doesn't fit well with our hurry-up, drive-thru, fast-food lifestyle. Under normal, healthy circumstances, we eat our meals in bite-sized portions, just as we climb every staircase and mountain one step at a time. Before we can have unity at the highest level, we must begin to climb the stairs of unity at the lowest level. This takes time, attention and life-changing effort; most of us think we have a critical shortage of the first two, so we neglect the third.

My concern is that we, as the members of His Church, have taken some dangerous shortcuts God never intended for us to take. We have attempted to leap over the first mandatory steps toward unity—those we are required to take in the relative obscurity of our homes and our closest, most private relationships. Our shortsighted goal has been to advance quickly to the more visible—and perhaps more glamorous—upper tiers of corporate unity.

It is a dangerous thing to climb a tower built on faulty foundations to gain the approval of men, pretending that we arrived at that great height of accomplishment wisely and legitimately. All it takes is one hypocritical wave of the praises of men and our tower of deception can suddenly destabilize and everything will come crashing down.

I am tired of so-called unity that is nothing more than a shallow outer shell of public statements and apparent like-mindedness—unity that is really built on the shaky foundations of mutual benefit and the unrealistic relationships of opportunism.

We can never achieve unity as God defines it by building it on the worldly what's-in-it-for-me approach to relationships. Nor can we build unity on a highly visible public level while neglecting or avoiding the critical issues causing disunity and separation on the hidden lower levels.

For instance, some people strive to maintain a continuous unity among their friends even as their family is unraveling at the seams. This is what happens when Dad keeps his appointment with the bowling team every Friday while his daughter stays home, shooting up drugs and wondering if her father really cares about her. When Mom gets so involved with local church activities and community service clubs that she only has time to tuck in Junior once or twice a week, a collapse of some kind is in the making. The time may come when she will wonder why Junior's grades have dipped so suddenly and why his behavior has changed so drastically.

If we can ever learn to apply our energy where disunity begins, instead of the place where it shows up in public, we will no longer be applying temporary Band-Aids as cosmetic cover-ups for potentially terminal wounds. Instead, we will begin healing our wounds and the wounds of others.

God placed an eternal longing and ache of the soul within each one of us. Our first great sense of relief comes the moment we surrender all and receive Him in our hearts—yet a lingering ache still remains. It is not because the saving work of Christ was incomplete; it is because *our* work is incomplete.

Jesus prayed that we would be one as He is one with the Father. In those few words our Savior described the source of our pain. We desperately miss the union with one another and with our Creator that we were created to enjoy! And we are not the only ones feeling the pain.

The unsaved world is constantly looking and hoping for some evidence that there really is a God in heaven. The lost are longing to see the slightest proof that the claims of Jesus Christ are true, and you and I are the key to it all. Jesus voiced the deepest longing of both God and man when He prayed that we would "be made perfect in one"[4] and that the world may know that the Father sent the Son and loves them as the Father loves His only Son.

It is time to become the answer to God's prayer and confirm the world's hope by demonstrating the unity Jesus enjoys with His Father. Let us follow the Prince of Peace on the path to unity with one another and with our Father. It all begins with a first step.

Notes
1. John 17:11, emphasis mine.
2. Prov. 18:24.
3. John 15:15.
4. John 17:23.

BECOMING PART OF THE ANSWER

The personal journal you hold in your hands was conceived in the mind of God long before I entered this world. Later He caused it to be birthed in prayer through my life, long before I knew I was going to write it and probably before you ever heard of Tommy Tenney. My point is that this journal wasn't printed by accident or created to be just another product to sell to Christians. It exists for one purpose: *to help you become an answer to God's prayer.*

Don't plan on simply scanning the individual readings and jotting down a few words before you rush on to the next page. You don't become an answer to God's prayer on the pray-as-you-drive, worship-on-the-go plan.

Prayerfully meditate on the biblical truths in the following pages and allow this journal to become a tool of the Holy Spirit in your life. I pray it will help move you to live in new levels of intimacy with the Lord Jesus Christ.

GOD IS CALLING US TO COME TOGETHER AROUND HIS THRONE

Every believer's personal goal should be to *live in the presence of the Lord every day*. My hope is that *Answering God's Prayer* will help you reach that goal. I am not interested in simply adding another pleasant teaching to a "gospel feed bag" that is already overstuffed and spilling over. No, you are reading these pages because I am convinced that God wants you and me and each of His children to come closer to Him and, in so doing, to draw closer to our families, our friends and the whole of the Body of Christ around His throne.

This journal was written specifically for individual use, but it may also be used for Christian marriage courses, Sunday School classes and Bible studies, although it will require more of you than simple study activities. You will find this journal to be most effective when used as a personal application workbook in conjunction with the book *God's Dream Team: A Call to Unity* (Ventura, CA: Regal Books, 1999), from which I have liberally quoted.

I must warn you that for this journal to be effective, you must spend some time *thinking*. I have found nothing more intellectually challenging than meditating on God's eternal Word. You will also need to *search your heart* and have the honesty and courage to face what you find there.

Please understand that the only reason I can write this journal is because God has taken me on this journey, too. I am still reaping a harvest from the seeds He helped me plant during that journey of the soul.

Nothing written on paper can truly affect lives in reality unless the ideas and concepts behind those words are *applied* to our everyday lives. This is especially true for any work based on God's Word. James the apostle sternly warned us in his New Testament epistle, "But be ye doers of the word, and not hearers only."[1] That is the very heart of this journey: We are out to do nothing less than to answer God's prayer for unity in the Church. Needless to say, that will take a whole lot more *doing* than *talking*.

BEGINNING YOUR JOURNEY

You will notice that the pages of this journal are not dated or linked with particular days of the week or month. I did this because few of us have the opportunity for a quiet time of meditation and personal contemplation every day. With that in mind, make sure that when you do get to pick up *Answering God's Prayer*, you pull away from the distractions of the day so you can give yourself completely to prayer and biblical meditation upon God's Word.

The biblical truths contained in this journal will make the greatest impact on your life when you take the time to allow the Holy Spirit to move in your heart and speak to you. He is the great Teacher; I am just a servant. He is able to take you beyond the letter of the Word and into the spirit of God's Word. Don't fall into the religious trap of simply making this journal a part of a daily regimen of religious duty.

Begin by finding a quiet place where you can be alone with your Bible, your journal and your Lord. Read each day's selection several times and make sure that you have captured the heart of what is being said. Do not settle for a quick read-through and a hurried jump to the next reading.

Allow the Spirit of God to enter your thought processes and bring fresh insight. Let the words that He brings to mind become a prayer from the heart. I realize that this practice of contemplative prayer has become a lost art in our Western society. We are used to having our spiritual food prepared, packaged, warmed up in the microwave of a high-powered worship service and delivered to our table by our favorite preacher-of-the-day. This journal represents your chance to break out of the spiritual fast-food rut.

The *Answering God's Prayer* journal is all about seeking and developing unity and cooperation among God's people to fulfill His dream for His Church. It is only logical, therefore, that I encourage you to talk to your friends about the ideas and concepts you encounter in these pages. Seek your friends' thoughts and reactions. You might consider memorizing phrases or passages that touch your heart so you can think on them throughout the day.

Come back to these readings often. This is healthy spiritual food, so don't be afraid to come back again and again for more. My hope is that each new day will bring fresh meaning, revelation and ideas for practical application in your life and in your church.

As you read, ask yourself these questions to help guide you in your journey to become part of the answer to God's prayer:

1. What is the main focus and intent behind the words of this passage?
2. How does this concept apply to my life?
3. What Scripture verses will help me apply this truth to my life in new or better ways?
4. What circumstances in my life enrich and illuminate the meaning of these statements?
5. Do I need to adjust any specific areas of my life to move closer to God and experience the power of this truth?
6. Is there anything in my life that prevents me from experiencing the reality of these powerful thoughts?
7. How can I incorporate the truths of this reading into a personal prayer to the Lord?

Allow me to launch our voyage into deeper obedience to God's Word with a thought from a God chaser named C. S. Lewis, who went to be with the Lord in 1963. One of the most important Christian thinkers in the twentieth century, Lewis wrote a penetrating work of Christian apologetics entitled *Mere Christianity*, which continues to touch millions of lives more than three decades after his death. This passage impacted me so much that I placed it in my *God Chasers Daily Meditation and Personal Journal*. I feel it bears repeating.

> Christ says, "Give Me all. . . . I have not come to torment your natural self, but to kill it. No half-measures are any good. I don't want to cut off a branch here and a branch there. I want to have the whole thing down."
>
> And the first job each morning consists simply in shoving [all your wishes and hopes] back; in listening to that other voice, taking that other point of view, letting that other larger, stronger, quieter life come flowing in.
>
> We can only do it for moments at first.[2]

Notes
1. Jas. 1:22, *KJV*.
2. C. S. Lewis, *Mere Christianity*, quoted in Tommy Tenney, *God Chasers Daily Meditation and Personal Journal* (Shippensburg, PA: Destiny Image, 1999), p. 36.

PART 1

PRESERVING THE MIDDLE GROUND

The path to unity isn't found by looking man in the face. *It is found by looking in the face of God.* The cherubim above the mercy seat of the Ark of the Covenant didn't look at each other because their sole focus was upon the *middle ground* between them—it was there that the blue flame of God's manifest presence pulsated and glowed.

True unity is found by mutually seeking God's face within the middle ground of holy habitation. Jesus' prayer that His disciples may be one isn't about me and it isn't about you. It is about preserving the middle ground between us where we meet God Himself. He will draw us together as we behold His glory—*this is what the fight is about!*

I have a vivid childhood memory of the time I walked up to a playground scuffle and asked the two bruised combatants, "What's the fight about?" Christianity is rife with examples of military terminology mixed with a dose of religiosity—from the phrase "Have you got the victory?" to more blatant terms such as "spiritual warfare." Most Christians understand that life is a battlefield; but whether they are new in the faith or seasoned veterans, many admit they don't really understand what the fight is about.

Unfortunately, this lack of understanding falls under God's prophetic declaration in Hosea: "My people are destroyed for lack of knowledge."[1] Soldiers who find themselves in a battle, with no idea of whom or what they are fighting against, can become their own worst enemy. The Church is in the same position as American troops on the front lines in Desert Storm: In the heat of battle we are quick to fire but slow to confirm our target. The result is that we often wound our own or are wounded by friendly fire—wounds inflicted by our friends.

In the Old Testament two people would "cut covenant" by splitting a calf, goat or ram into two pieces and passing between the halves together while repeating the words "The Lord be between you and me." This was the most serious and solemn agreement two people—or God and man—could make with one another. A covenant could bring great blessings and security to those in the agreement; but it could also bring a deadly curse to anyone who broke a covenant made while walking between the sacrifices.[2]

When God promised to make Abram the father of many nations and to give him the Promised Land, Abram asked, "Lord GOD, how shall I know that I will inherit it?"[3] God responded by making a covenant with him. He told Abram to bring Him a heifer (a young cow that has never given birth to a calf), a she-goat and a ram, along with a turtledove and a young pigeon. Abram cut everything in half except for the birds—signifying that the Holy Spirit can never be divided—and placed each side opposite the other.

SATAN ALWAYS WANTS TO DESTROY THE MIDDLE GROUND

Throughout the daylight hours, Abram drove away vultures that tried to steal any of the sacrifices arranged in two rows. I'm sure Abram thought that his primary battle was to preserve the carcasses, but there was much more at stake than he could ever imagine! That the vultures or buzzards symbolize Satan and his dark hosts may seem obvious. What is *not* so apparent is the fact that Satan wasn't merely trying to steal the sacrifice. *He wanted to destroy the middle ground*—the place of meeting between God and man.

Abram (like most Christians today) didn't realize that whether Satan got one half of the carcass or the other didn't matter—either side would do. The adversary knew then, and he knows now, that when one is taken away, there is no more middle ground. If just one of the cherubim were removed from the top of the Ark, there would be no mercy seat. Remember that God said, "And there I will meet with you, and I will speak with you from above the mercy seat, from *between* the two cherubim which are on the ark of the Testimony."[4]

This is what the fight is about. It's about *preserving a meeting place* for man to encounter God. The size of the "between zone"—the middle ground—will determine the size of the visitation. Your first priority, my first priority, *our* first priority must be to carve out an open space, a place for God to meet with us. It doesn't matter how busy our schedules may be.

IS THERE A MIDDLE GROUND FOR GOD IN YOUR FAMILY?

We can't have a visitation of holy fire collectively or corporately until we have it on an individual, personal level. We need Him at every level of our existence. How much room have you created for God to appear in your life? Is there a middle ground prepared and preserved for Him in your family? Is there any place reserved for Him in your community? How much room is available for Him in the life of your church? Of all of the churches in your region?

THE LORD BE BETWEEN YOU AND ME

When Jonathan and David reluctantly parted for the last time, they said to one another, "The LORD be between you and me."[5] Ancient Jewish covenants were traditionally sealed with these most solemn of words. The Hebrew word translated as "between" in this statement actually means middle. Jesus affirmed this middle ground as the place where God meets us when He said, "For where two or three are gathered together in My name, *I am there in the midst [middle] of them.*"[6]

God doesn't come to you, and He doesn't come to me. *He comes between us* so that *all of us* can touch Him but none of us control Him. He always searches for the middle ground.

The middle ground shows up wherever we find God dealing with men. When Jesus died at Golgotha, where do we find Him in His final moments, declaring to His Father "It is finished"?[7] He died on the middle cross between two men—one representing the repentant, the other representing the unrepentant. The Son of Man laid down His life suspended between earth and the third heaven, as though unworthy of both. It was on the middle ground that the Sacrificed Lamb shed His blood and sealed His own covenant to destroy the power of the curse of death and the grave over the human race. Middle ground is holy ground!

Abram faithfully chased away the vultures until nightfall, when God Himself came and stood between the rows of sacrifices like a burning lamp of fire. This was unusual, because normally the two people who were cutting a covenant would pass through the sacrifices together. In His covenant with Abram, God swore by Himself "because He could swear by no one greater."[8] Then God passed alone between the carcasses on the middle ground. (I wonder if God put Abram to sleep so he wouldn't try to stand on the middle ground with God's holiness? It may have destroyed him had he tried.)

Since God swore by Himself, even if Abram faltered in believing, the covenant could never fail. The covenant was based on God's faithfulness, not man's weakness. When the Son of God died on the cross on the middle ground, He also made covenant with Himself.

THERE ARE TWO THINGS WE CAN DO

There appear to be two things we can do to help create this middle ground where God can visit: We can worship Him and we can come into anointed agreement.

These things may not seem to be a big deal to many who read this paragraph. *I've heard that sermon before*, you may be thinking. *Yeah, I studied that at a worship seminar a couple of years ago—it's good stuff, but I'm ready for some* deep *teaching.* Before we bypass worship and unity as boring subjects, perhaps we should ask ourselves why worship and unity are important enough to attract both the attention of God and the hindering activity of Satan.

The Bible says, "But You are holy, enthroned in the praises of Israel."[9] This was written by King David, a man who literally sat before the Ark of the Covenant in a tabernacle without walls or a veil. At times he gazed all night long at the flickering blue flame of God's *shekinah* glory resting in the middle of the mercy seat between the cherubim. Writing under the inspiration of the Holy Spirit, the psalmist tells us our worship literally builds a throne for God in the middle of our praises! No wonder the enemy hates our praises so vehemently.

Jesus, speaking of unity among the brethren, said:

Again I say to you that if two of you agree on earth concerning anything that they ask, it will be done for them by My Father in heaven. For where two or three are gathered together in My name, I am there in the [middle ground between] them.[10]

SATAN DOESN'T CARE ABOUT US— HE HATES THE MIDDLE GROUND

When Satan comes to hinder or attack the brethren, he isn't really after you or me. He couldn't care less about any single one of us; he just wants to remove one side or the other of the equation of unified sacrifice of praise and worship. By doing so, *he destroys the place of visitation*—the middle ground of unity.

Why is Satan so fixated on destroying the middle ground? Is it because that is the one place he can never go again? He was once known as Lucifer, the covering cherub and angel of light who literally covered the center of the whole universe—the throne of God—with continuous worship and praise. Once Lucifer (literally, the Morning Star) rebelled against God, he was stripped of his name and given the moniker of "Satan," which means attack or adversary. He and the angels who followed him were ejected from that blessed place.

Since Satan can never return to that heavenly place and position of worship again, he wants to prevent *our* unified praise and worship from creating a throne for God on earth. For one thing, that fallen cherub knows firsthand what happens when the Almighty takes His seat, enthroned in divine power in the middle ground between sacrificial worshippers! *The archrebel fears that place of visitation and habitation more than any other.*

When we worship God in spirit and in truth, He comes between us, or "in our midst." The Old Testament pictures God dwelling above the mercy seat where the wings of the cherubim touched. In the New Testament, Jesus promised to come between or among us where two or three are gathered together in His name. In agreement and sacrificial worship together, we can literally create a New Testament "throne zone"—the heavenly seat where we gather in agreement around the centrality of Christ—the place of divine visitation where anything is possible!

If You Build It, He Will Come

The fight is on, and this time we know what it's about. It's about seeing His will done on earth and in us as it is in heaven. It is time for you and me to make room—to create a middle ground of worship and unity of heart, mind and body. Our God has a throne in heaven, but He is seeking a throne surrounded by the sacrifices of praise and unified worship of those who seek Him because they freely choose to. Our goal in the battle is simple: If we build it, He will come. Once we build a mercy seat, we will discover that there is divine provision in God's presence.

David's life reveals another key truth about God's ways and unity in the Kingdom. You can either enter the court of the king through *political position*—when David married Saul's daughter and assumed command of Israel's armies, he appeared to be going that route—or you can enter it through the *worship position*.

David emerged from God's presence in the hills near Bethlehem to save his nation when he was just a teenager. However, he entered Saul's royal court through man's favor and the privileges and position of marriage. Then God slammed shut the door of political advancement and said, "No, David. You don't enter the kind of kingdom I'm talking about through political position. You enter it through a worship position."

Years later, after David was crowned king of Israel, he began to pursue God's presence and returned the Ark of the Covenant to Jerusalem. His wife, Saul's daughter Michal, openly rejected David and his passion for God's presence. She wanted a man who excelled in political position as her father had. David had left politics and the favor of men far behind. He was pursuing the kingdom through a worship position, no matter what the cost. Michal remained a barren woman the rest of her life, but David went on to become Israel's greatest king, prophet and psalmist.

We can count on paying a price when we change our focus from the approval of men to the pursuit of God's presence and the unity of the brethren; but the benefits far outweigh the cost. Most of David's adult life was focused on two vital goals: First, he wanted to return God's glory to his city and nation and build a place of divine habitation, not merely visitation. Second, David worked unceasingly to bring unity of purpose, heart and worship to his divided nation.

David's quest began and ended in the middle ground of God's presence, the place where God and man commune in the intimate atmosphere of sacrificial worship and adoration of the real King. Israel enjoyed her greatest days under David's leadership. It was only when Solomon and Israel turned their eyes away from God's presence toward the distractions of worldly things and other gods that their unity and their nation were divided and ultimately destroyed.

THE PURSUIT OF GOD'S PRESENCE

I want to share some thoughts drawn from one of my favorite wells of godly wisdom, the writings of A. W. Tozer. A man of deep prayer and a fervent, lifelong God chaser, Tozer offers us some probing insights into the role of unity in revival and the visitation of God. The following excerpt is taken from his book *Paths to Power*:

Oneness of Mind. God always works where His people meet His conditions, but only when and as they do. Any spiritual visitation will be limited or extensive, depending on how well and how widely conditions are met. The first condition is oneness of mind among the persons who are seeking the visitation. "Behold, how good and how pleasant it is for brethren to dwell together in unity! It is like the precious ointment upon the head, that ran down upon the beard, even Aaron's beard: that went down to the skirts of his garments; as the dew of Hermon, and as the dew that descended upon the mountains of Zion: for there the LORD commanded the blessing, even life for evermore" (Ps. 133, *KJV*). Here the unity precedes the blessing, and so it is throughout the Bible. An individual may seek and obtain great spiritual help from God, and that is one thing. For a company of people to unite to seek a new visitation from God for the entire group is quite another thing, and is a spiritual labor greatly superior to the first. The one is a personal affair, and may easily begin and end with a single person; the other may go on to bless unlimited numbers of persons.

It can hardly be doubted that there are many Spirit-filled persons, living pure devoted lives, who nevertheless exercise little or no power in the direction of revival. They live in beautiful isolation, doing nothing to bring down "showers of blessing" upon the larger group. Such as these have given up to the spirit of the times and have ceased to expect revival tides. They hear Jesus say, "Let down the hook and line for a fish," rather than, "Let down the net for a draught."

There is such a thing as a flow of blessing, where one experience merges into another, one day's grace moves on to the next. The spiritual mood persists from one meeting to the next, permitting the Spirit to advance His work. It eliminates the discouraging necessity to repeat each Sunday the work done the week before. It gives the high benefit of accumulation and serves to attract increasing numbers to the fountain. It is this we need today.

Historically, revivals have been mainly the achieving of a oneness of mind among a number of Christian believers. In the second chapter of Acts it is recorded that they were "all with one accord in one place" when the Spirit came upon them. He did not come to bring them into oneness of accord; He came because they were already so. The Spirit never comes to give unity (though His presence certainly aids and perfects such unity as may exist). He comes to that company who have, through repentance and faith, brought their hearts into one accord.

The Doctrine of Passivity. This may disturb some who have not stopped to question the commonly accepted doctrine that unity of heart among Christians is a sovereign work of God, and that we can have no part in it. This dull doctrine of inaction has taught us that we should study to do nothing and hope vaguely that somehow God will bring us to oneness of accord. If the achieving of unity is solely a work of God, why are we constantly exhorted to unity by Christ and His apostles? "Fulfil ye my joy, that ye be likeminded, having the same love, being of one accord, of one mind" (Phil. 2:2, *KJV*). "Endeavouring to keep the unity of the Spirit in the bond of peace" (Eph. 4:3, *KJV*). "I beseech Euodias, and beseech Syntyche, that they be of the same mind in the Lord" (Phil. 4:2, *KJV*). "Now I beseech you, brethren, by the name of our Lord Jesus Christ, that ye all speak the same thing, and that there be no divisions among you; but that ye be perfectly joined together in the same mind and in the same judgment" (1 Cor. 1:10, *KJV*). It is plain from all this that believers have a large part in achieving and maintaining unity among themselves. In this as in everything else God must give effective aid, but He cannot do the work alone. He must have active cooperation on the part of the believer. And since the Holy Spirit can do His mighty works only where unity exists, it becomes of utmost importance that everyone who desires revival do everything in his power to bring about such a state of unity on as wide a scale as possible.

An Objection Answered. Now, it is easy to find in this teaching a source of discouragement for the struggling pastor. "If oneness of accord is so important to the working of the Spirit, then I despair of my church. Its members are made up of a cross section of Protestantism, with a dozen shades of theological opinion among them. They agree on the fundamentals, it is true, but they differ on so many points that I could never hope to bring them together. How can they erase the differences arising from varying religious backgrounds? How can they ever see eye to eye on all points? If God cannot send refreshing until we have accomplished what I believe to be the impossible, then our case is hopeless." Something like this will be the reply to our exhortation to unity, and the troubled soul who thus states his case will be no opposer, but a sincere lover of God and men.

This argument would seem to destroy all that has been said in favor of revival unity were it not for two facts: (1) The oneness of which we speak is not theological oneness; (2) unity embracing one hundred percent of the people is not required before God begins to work. God responds to even "two or three" who may be gathered in His name; *the extent and power of His working will depend upon the size of the nucleus* with relation to the total number of believers in church.

Revival Unity. Revival unity is not the same as doctrinal unity. God demands no more than oneness in all things that matter; in all other things we are free to think as we will. The disciples at Pentecost were one only in the things of the Spirit; in everything else they were one hundred and twenty. Harmony may be defined as oneness at points of contact. It need extend no further than this to meet the requirements of revival. God will bless a body of men and women who are one in spiritual purpose, even if their doctrinal positions are not identical on every point. Then, we should be encouraged to know that God does not wait for perfection in any church. A smaller group within the larger body may be the key to the revival. They who compose this group need only become united in heart and purpose and God will begin a work in them, a work which may go on to embrace larger numbers as they meet the simple conditions. The greater the number in any church who are of one heart and one mind the more powerfully will the Spirit move in His work of salvation; but He never waits for an every-member participation. Every church should strive for unity among its members, not languidly, but earnestly and optimistically. Every pastor should show his people the possibilities for power that lie in this fusion of many souls into one.[11]

Unity at every level is a blessed byproduct of seeking the face of God more than merely seeking His hand for His benefits. We must resist the pressure to create temporary covenants of man-made unity by gazing into the eyes of men and relying on slipshod alliances founded on common likes and dislikes.

True unity can only come with the gaze of the cherubim and the creation and preservation of the middle ground. For some time I have been saying, "In revival, the size of the middle ground determines the size of the visitation." I later learned that A. W. Tozer saw this as well and wrote of it. This only reinforces my determination to pursue God's presence in the unity of the middle ground with other brothers and sisters, for I long for His habitation, not merely a momentary visitation.

We must fix our eyes, our hearts and our hopes on the King of glory and offer Him sacrifices of praise and worship. As we labor together to enthrone Him upon our praises, He will come and make us one, and we will have answered the heart's desire of God Himself.

Notes
1. Hos. 4:6.
2. See Jer. 34:18-22.
3. Gen. 15:8.
4. Exod. 25:22, emphasis mine.
5. 1 Sam. 20:23.
6. Matt. 18:20, emphasis mine.

7. John 19:30.
8. Heb. 6:13.
9. Ps. 22:3.
10. Matt. 18:19,20.
11. A. W. Tozer, *Paths to Power* (Camp Hill, PA: Christian Publications, n.d.), pp. 59-64, emphasis mine. Used with permission.

PART 2

THE PRESCRIPTION FOR UNITY

The physical body is an engineering masterpiece: a physiological and biochemical wonder. It has incredible strength, endurance and abilities, yet it can easily suffer injury from accidents, disease or misuse. The same is true of the earthly Body of Christ, the Church.

When the delicate balance of her parts and functions is disturbed or disrupted, we must turn to the counsel of the Creator, who framed and formed the Church, and to the Great Physician, who maintains and preserves her health.

Nothing brings a certain cure to spiritual and relational sickness like God's prescription for unity.

CREATED EQUAL BUT DIFFERENT: WE ARE COMMANDED TO WALK TOGETHER

Insight for the Heart

We must learn to understand that even though the United States Constitution declares that all men are created equal, this does not mean we are all identical. We must learn to accept our differences, without making wars out of minor disagreements.

In Ephesians, when Paul spoke of "forbearing one another in love,"[1] one writer interpreted this passage to mean "steadily pouring yourselves out for each other in acts of love, alert at noticing differences and quick at mending fences. You were all called to travel on the same road and in the same direction, so stay together, both outwardly and inwardly."[2] (*God's Dream Team*, p. 60.)

Applications for Life

1. How does this "equal but different" concept apply to the Godhead and the Church's leadership gifts mentioned in Ephesians 4:11,12?

2. How does it apply to your relationships?

Note
1. Eph. 4:2, *KJV*.
2. Eph. 4:2-4, *THE MESSAGE*.

Dear Dreamkeeper: This prayer focus is a small portion of the larger "Dreamkeeper's Prayer" which is adapted from Appendix C of *God's Dream Team* on pages 144 and 145. Each series of seven readings will focus on one of the ten parts of the larger prayer. At the end of the readings we will pray the entire prayer as a way of dedicating ourselves individually and corporately to the task of answering God's prayer that we may be one in Jesus Christ.

_____

_____

_____

_____

_____

_____

_____

_____

_____

_____

_____

_____

_____

_____

_____

_____

_____

_____

_____

_____

_____

_____

| THE DREAMKEEPER'S PRAYER FOCUS, PART 1 |

Lord, we long to answer Your prayer for unity
so that the world will know You are the Son of God
and that You have come from the Father.
Yet I know the "we" must begin with me.

DON'T SAY YOU LOVE ME UNLESS YOU ARE READY TO DIE FOR ME

Insight for the Heart

If we want to identify biblical love, we should look for *sacrificial* love. We really can't say we love our neighbors until we are ready to die for them. We should say, "I would rather be crucified myself than see you go to hell."[1] God calls us to hate the sin while loving the sinner. Most of us prefer to do one thing at a time, so we work on hating both sin and sinner at the same time, or we love both the sinner and his deadly sin. (*God's Dream Team*, pp. 60, 61.)

Application for Life

1. Why is it easier for us to go to one of two extremes rather than obey God's command to love the sinner and hate the sin?

Note
1. See Rom. 9:3.

| THE DREAMKEEPER'S PRAYER FOCUS, PART 1 |

Lord, we long to answer Your prayer for unity
so that the world will know You are the Son of God
and that You have come from the Father.
Yet I know the "we" must begin with me.

IT IS TIME FOR MERCY ON THE COMMON DECK OF FAITH

Insight for the Heart

True unity is not achieved by leaving our differences hidden, but by dealing with them in the open air of Christ's mercy. Just as a ship has many cabins, so God's kingdom has room for many opinions. But just as a ship has only one main deck, it is on this common deck where we come out of our cabins to stand together.

This common deck, or common ground, represents the essentials of our faith, such as the uniqueness of Christ, the infallibility of Scripture, the substitutionary atonement. It is from this deck we face the world. I have brothers and sisters with whom I disagree on the role of women, the meaning of baptism, the place of millennialism. But our uncommon ground is a small, barren island compared to the great continent of common ground we share. If we can agree upon the majestic uniqueness of Christ, don't we share enough to accept one another?[1] (*God's Dream Team*, p. 61.)

Applications for Life

1. Have you stranded yourself on any barren islands of doctrine or belief lately?

2. Honestly, you don't have to give them up or compromise them if they are true. Now, will you accept God's rescue and rejoin the rest of the family on the mainland of Christ?

Note
1. Max Lucado, *Upwards* newsletter, n.d., n.p.

┌───┐
│ THE DREAMKEEPER'S PRAYER FOCUS, PART 1 │
└───┘

*Lord, we long to answer Your prayer for unity
so that the world will know You are the Son of God
and that You have come from the Father.
Yet I know the "we" must begin with me.*

SERVANTHOOD IS THE WOMB OF UNITY

Insight for the Heart

Only those with a servant's heart can birth unity. Servanthood is the womb in which unity is allowed to develop; arrogance is the birth canal of division. It is the searching and striving for preeminence among us that creates division. There is no room in the Church for a spirit of competition or a spirit of division. There is much room, though, for servants. Jesus always had an eye for that kind of people. (*God's Dream Team*, p. 62.)

Applications for Life

1. What kind of offspring is flourishing in your spiritual womb right now?

2. Will your "child" be called Unity, or will it be called Division? (You will know its name by the fruit it produces.)

3. Which one would Jesus rather embrace and call His own?

_____
_____
_____
_____
_____
_____
_____
_____
_____
_____
_____
_____
_____
_____
_____
_____
_____
_____
_____
_____
_____
_____

THE DREAMKEEPER'S PRAYER FOCUS, PART 1

Lord, we long to answer Your prayer for unity
so that the world will know You are the Son of God
and that You have come from the Father.
Yet I know the "we" must begin with me.

HAVE YOU DONE WELL? HAVE YOU BEEN FAITHFUL? HAVE YOU SERVED?

Insight for the Heart

No matter where we come from, if we walk through the pearly gates of heaven, we will enter as servants, because Jesus told us He will say "Well done, thou good and faithful servant."[1] Make no mistake: He won't say "Well done" if we have not done well. Nor will He say "faithful servant" if we haven't *served faithfully,* much less call us a "servant" if we haven't *served.* (*God's Dream Team,* p. 63.)

Applications for Life

1. Many of us manage to focus on only one thing at a time in our Christian walk. How do these three dimensions of servant-hood apply to the different areas of your life?

2. How well are you doing in these three areas? Who can help you do better? (There is One right answer.)

Note
1. Matt. 25:21, *KJV.*

_____

_____

_____

_____

_____

_____

_____

THE DREAMKEEPER'S PRAYER FOCUS, PART 1

*Lord, we long to answer Your prayer for unity
so that the world will know You are the Son of God
and that You have come from the Father.
Yet I know the "we" must begin with me.*

GLORY GIVEN AWAY IS BETTER THAN GLORY TREASURED

Insight for the Heart

On one particular day in a wealthy Pharisee's house, a woman entered the room uninvited and unwelcome. She washed Jesus' feet with her tears and dried them with her hair. According to Scripture, a woman's hair is her glory.[1] A true servant says, "My glory is only good enough to wash the animal dung off your feet." The disciples got pretty bent out of shape about the incident. But Jesus seemed to say, "I'll see that while they may forget the words that you spoke here, they will always remember what she did here."[2] (*God's Dream Team*, p. 63.)

Application for Life

1. How can you cause the Lord to remember what you *do* today more than the words you speak today?

Notes
1. See 1 Cor. 11:15.
2. See Matt. 26:13; Mark 14:9.

———————————————————

———————————————————

———————————————————

———————————————————

———————————————————

———————————————————

———————————————————

———————————————————

_____

_____

_____

_____

_____

_____

_____

_____

_____

_____

_____

_____

_____

_____

_____

_____

_____

_____

_____

_____

_____

_____

_____

_____

_____

| THE DREAMKEEPER'S PRAYER FOCUS, PART 1 |

Lord, we long to answer Your prayer for unity
so that the world will know You are the Son of God
and that You have come from the Father.
Yet I know the "we" must begin with me.

YOUR ABILITY TO CREATE UNITY IS DIRECTLY RELATED TO YOUR ABILITY TO BE A SERVANT

Insight for the Heart

There must be "Marys" among us—women and men who are unafraid to display the heart of a servant instead of an egotistical human spirit. We need "alabaster box breakers" who will not mind that what they say is not well remembered, but that what they do with a servant's heart is never forgotten. God's kingdom will be built by servants. (*God's Dream Team*, p. 63.)

Applications for Life

1. What is your "alabaster box"?

2. Are you willing to break it as a precious and fragrant offering to Jesus?

_____

_____

_____

_____

_____

_____

_____

_____

_____

_____
_____
_____
_____
_____
_____
_____
_____
_____
_____
_____
_____
_____
_____
_____
_____
_____
_____
_____
_____
_____
_____
_____
_____

THE DREAMKEEPER'S PRAYER FOCUS, PART 1

*Lord, we long to answer Your prayer for unity
so that the world will know You are the Son of God
and that You have come from the Father.
Yet I know the "we" must begin with me.*

WANTED: SERVANTS (SELF-PROMOTING CONTROLLERS NEED NOT APPLY)

Insight for the Heart

God does not need people to fight for Him; He needs people who will be servants. The principles of His kingdom will fight for themselves. The spirit of a servant is what will create unity. A servant does not care who is in control. A servant does not seek preeminence for himself but only seeks the furtherance of the kingdom of God. (*God's Dream Team*, p. 64.)

Applications for Life

1. God made each of us unique and different from one another. Are you naturally dominant (a born leader) or compliant (a born follower)?

2. How did you feel about the statements made above?

3. Regardless of your answer, are you willing to become a servant and lift Him above everything else in your life?

_____

_____

_____

_____

_____

_____

_____

_____
_____
_____
_____
_____
_____
_____
_____
_____
_____
_____
_____
_____
_____
_____
_____
_____
_____
_____
_____
_____

THE DREAMKEEPER'S PRAYER FOCUS, PART 2

I want to make You Lord of my life
and not merely call You Lord.
Holy Spirit, I ask You to convict and perfect me
so that I can accomplish what the Father has called me to do.

THE DOCTOR'S PRESCRIPTION FOR A REVIVAL OF UNITY

Insight for the Heart

Luke the physician gave us a prescription for revival in the book of Acts and he begins by referring to "my former book,"[1] or the Gospel of Luke. While the Gospel of Luke describes what *Jesus Christ* did, the book of Acts tells us what *we* should do.

The basic ingredient of the prescription is Christ. He is the owner and originator of the ointment of anointing. Beginning at the fourth chapter of Luke all the way through to the end, the first verse of every chapter talks about Jesus Christ, Jesus, Lord or a personal pronoun referring to Him. Jesus is Luke's main theme. Then He said, I am going to send the "promise of the Father [the Holy Ghost]."[2] Jesus made it clear that the Holy Spirit He was sending would lead and guide us.[3] (*God's Dream Team*, pp. 64, 65.)

Applications for Life

1. What is your main theme?

2. How does the role of the Holy Spirit after the Lord's resurrection relate to what He did before His death on Calvary?

3. Do you ask for the Holy Spirit's help each day?

Notes
1. Acts 1:1, *NIV*.
2. See 1 Cor. 11:15.
3. See John 14:26; 16:13.

_____

_____

_____

_____

_____

_____

_____

_____

_____

_____

_____

_____

_____

_____

_____

_____

_____

_____

_____

_____

_____

_____

_____

| THE DREAMKEEPER'S PRAYER FOCUS, PART 2 |

I want to make You Lord of my life
and not merely call You Lord.
Holy Spirit, I ask You to convict and perfect me
so that I can accomplish what the Father has called me to do.

I Am in the Father and the Father Is in Me

Insight for the Heart

Jesus our High Priest, working through the Holy Spirit, is still in charge of mixing the prescription for what ails us. Jesus displayed true unity while walking among us on the earth—He was and is *inseparable* from the Father. Supernatural unity includes the mystery of not being able to clearly see or know where He ends and the Father begins. (*God's Dream Team*, p. 65.)

Applications for Life

1. What does "being one" mean?

2. Are you inseparable from Christ and your Christian friends?

_____

_____

_____

_____

_____

_____

_____

_____

_____

_____

_____
_____
_____
_____
_____
_____
_____
_____
_____
_____
_____
_____
_____
_____
_____
_____
_____
_____
_____
_____
_____
_____
_____

THE DREAMKEEPER'S PRAYER FOCUS, PART 2

I want to make You Lord of my life
and not merely call You Lord.
Holy Spirit, I ask You to convict and perfect me
so that I can accomplish what the Father has called me to do.

UNITY MADE THE "SUDDENLY" POSSIBLE

Insight for the Heart

The prescription was nearly complete by the Day of Pentecost. The disciples were waiting in submitted obedience to the Lord's command, and they were of one mind and one accord. Jesus was present in their midst because their unity made it possible for Him to continue what He had begun to do and teach. He answered their unity with a "suddenly" from heaven![1] (*God's Dream Team*, p. 65.)

Applications for Life

1. Would you like to experience the "suddenly" visitation of God in your life?

2. How can you personally apply the keys of unity and submitted waiting?

Note
1. Acts 2:2; see Acts 1:14; 2:46.

_____

_____

_____

_____

_____

_____

_____

_____

_____

_____

_____

_____

_____

_____

_____

_____

_____

_____

_____

_____

_____

_____

_____

_____

_____

_____

_____

_____

_____

THE DREAMKEEPER'S PRAYER FOCUS, PART 2

*I want to make You Lord of my life
and not merely call You Lord.
Holy Spirit, I ask You to convict and perfect me
so that I can accomplish what the Father has called me to do.*

ARE YOU WILLING TO TAKE YOUR MEDICINE?

Insight for the Heart

Jesus Christ must be supreme in our lives. If He is the originator and the owner, then His commandments need to be the focal point of our lives. He said, "If you love Me you will love your brother."[1] In John's Gospel, Jesus said, "By this all will know that you are My disciples, if you have love for one another"[2] and "I and My Father are one."[3] If we are to follow His prescription, we must come to the place where we can honestly say "I and my brother are one." (*God's Dream Team*, p. 65.)

Applications for Life

1. Do you wish you could pick and choose which brothers or sisters with whom you will be one?

2. Since you can't, what *will* you do?

Note
1. See 1 John 4:21.
2. John 13:35.
3. John 10:30, *KJV*.

_____

_____

_____

_____

_____

_____

_____

_____

_____

_____

_____

_____

_____

_____

_____

_____

_____

_____

_____

_____

_____

_____

| THE DREAMKEEPER'S PRAYER FOCUS, PART 2 |

I want to make You Lord of my life
and not merely call You Lord.
Holy Spirit, I ask You to convict and perfect me
so that I can accomplish what the Father has called me to do.

HAS SOMEONE TAMPERED WITH YOUR PRESCRIPTION?

Insight for the Heart

If confusion reigns [in a supposed move of God], then we are sure of one thing: God is not the author of it.[1] If disunity is displayed, it did not come from above; it came from beneath—either in the hellish realm or the human realm. Somebody is *tampering with the prescription*. There's a fly in the ointment. It is critical for us to understand that God is not the author of confusion; He is the author of peace. (*God's Dream Team*, p. 65.)

Applications for Life

1. As you think about your life, your home and your local church body, do you see evidence of confusion, disunity or unity at work?

2. Now that you see it, what is your role in what happens next?

Note
1. See 1 Cor. 14:33.

_____

_____

_____

_____

_____

_____

_____

_____

_____

_____

_____

_____

_____

_____

_____

_____

_____

_____

_____

_____

_____

_____

_____

_____

_____

_____

_____

_____

_____

_____

THE DREAMKEEPER'S PRAYER FOCUS, PART 2

I want to make You Lord of my life
and not merely call You Lord.
Holy Spirit, I ask You to convict and perfect me
so that I can accomplish what the Father has called me to do.

THE ART OF MAKING GOOD MEDICINE

Insight for the Heart

The Lord is not so concerned with *what you do for Him* as He is with *how you do it*. If your service is rendered from a servant's heart, it will bring unity in the Body.

Scripturally, we are all to be mutually submitted to one another as servants. When the ministry becomes the servant of the people and the people become the servants of the ministry and of each other, true biblical unity is achieved. As the deacons served the apostles by lifting the load and doing things that they could do, freeing the apostles to do the things that only they could do, they created the prescription. (*God's Dream Team*, p. 66.)

Application for Life

1. In the terminology of this reading, what kind of prescription have you been creating with your life—good medicine or bad medicine?

_____

_____

_____

_____

_____

_____

_____

_____

_____

_____

_____

_____

_____

_____

_____

_____

_____

_____

_____

_____

_____

_____

_____

_____

_____

_____

_____

_____

_____

_____

THE DREAMKEEPER'S PRAYER FOCUS, PART 2

I want to make You Lord of my life
and not merely call You Lord.
Holy Spirit, I ask You to convict and perfect me
so that I can accomplish what the Father has called me to do.

WHO'S REALLY IN CONTROL? (AND WHY DO YOU ASK?)

Insight for the Heart

Our problem is that we are still struggling with the cancer of control. Who's in control? We fail to realize that God is ultimately in control. Because He started it and we are to continue it doesn't mean that He is abandoning His leadership and supremacy in all things. (*God's Dream Team*, pp. 66, 67.)

In other words, whose car is it? Whether we are talking about the local church, the Church universal or the breath you just took, it all belongs to God. We need to release our death grip on the steering wheel and let Him take control of every aspect of our lives, homes and ministries. Things will go a whole lot better if we start worrying less and praying more.

Applications for Life

1. Do you ever get frustrated with those who lead in your church or in nationally visible ministries?

2. If God really is big enough to clean up any messes His people make, how should your attitude about flawed leaders be affected (that includes *all* of them)?

_____

_____

_____

_____

_____

_____

| THE DREAMKEEPER'S PRAYER FOCUS, PART 3 |

Grant me, and grant us, the grace to walk in humility,
considering others better than ourselves.
May we look after the interests of others
as carefully as we look after our own.
Above all, may my attitude be the same as Yours—
that of a humble servant.

A SPECIAL PRESCRIPTION FOR THOSE WHO WANT TO BE FIRST

Insight for the Heart

Unity brings about an incredible amount of power. Some people think the only path to power is to put people *under you*, never understanding that the real path to power is to put Jesus Christ *over you* and become a servant to those *around you*. He said, "And whosoever of you will be the chiefest, shall be servant of all."[1] (*God's Dream Team*, p. 67.)

Applications for Life

1. What is the fastest route to the "top" in God's kingdom—to climb or to dive?

2. How does your personal track record look right now? (Don't worry, most of us take a hard fall at this point.)

Note
1. Mark 10:44, *KJV.*

_____

_____

_____

_____

_____

_____

_____

_____

_____

_____

_____

_____

_____

_____

_____

_____

_____

_____

_____

_____

_____

_____

_____

_____

_____

_____

_____

_____

_____

_____

_____

_____

THE DREAMKEEPER'S PRAYER FOCUS, PART 3

Grant me, and grant us, the grace to walk in humility,
considering others better than ourselves.
May we look after the interests of others
as carefully as we look after our own.
Above all, may my attitude be the same as Yours—
that of a humble servant.

DO YOU ATTEND THE FIRST CHURCH OF THE STENCH OF SIN OR THE HUMBLE CHURCH OF FRAGRANT SERVANTHOOD?

Insight for the Heart

I wonder how many of us are like the disciples—sitting around the room with our dirty, smelly, self-righteous (and self-willed) feet, trying to pretend nothing stinks. We act like we really believe all is perfect in the Church and we can't understand why people don't want to come to where we are. Yet when sinners walk into a room full of stinking Christian self-righteousness and the unpleasant odors of unholy attitudes, they walk right back out. You see, the stench of sin is so strong in their world that they don't want anything that even has a hint of its fragrance lingering about it. They want the Church to smell different, to act different, to be different from the world in which they live. What a difference when a church is full of humility, when someone has taken the cloth and the basin and begun to wash the dirt and grime from their brother's feet! Sometimes God has more problems with the self-righteous than the unrighteous. (*God's Dream Team*, p. 72.)

Applications for Life

1. How do your spiritual feet smell right now?

2. Which is the better cure for stinking attitudes—a good foot-washing or the humble act of washing the feet of others?

_____

_____

_____

_____

_____

_____

_____

_____

_____

_____

_____

_____

_____

_____

_____

_____

_____

_____

_____

_____

_____

_____

_____

THE DREAMKEEPER'S PRAYER FOCUS, PART 3

Grant me, and grant us, the grace to walk in humility,
considering others better than ourselves.
May we look after the interests of others
as carefully as we look after our own.
Above all, may my attitude be the same as Yours—
that of a humble servant.

SHOE-SHINE SERVANTHOOD

Insight for the Heart

We must understand that servanthood is a unity builder. It puts things together. Again:

> *Your ability to create unity is directly related to your ability to be a servant.*

I began to understand this principle of servanthood as a young man in my father's house. One night I devised a plan whereby I could stay up late to listen in on the living-room conversations between preachers. Shortly before my bedtime, I quietly collected all the ministers' shoes, sat in a corner and diligently began to polish their shoes. I was slow and deliberate, ostensibly to do a very good job (which I did), but realistically to prolong my "listening" time. My father couldn't bring himself to force me to go to bed.

Almost by accident I discovered the secret path of servanthood and was allowed to linger longer, like Joshua, around the things of God. That's when I felt my ministry was birthed—when I started shining shoes. (*God's Dream Team*, pp. 72, 73.)

Application for Life

1. Are there some "shoes" in the corners of your life that you need to polish for the sake of lingering or for the preservation of unity? (Either motive is acceptable.)

THE DREAMKEEPER'S PRAYER FOCUS, PART 3

Grant me, and grant us, the grace to walk in humility,
considering others better than ourselves.
May we look after the interests of others
as carefully as we look after our own.
Above all, may my attitude be the same as Yours—
that of a humble servant.

ARE YOU A SWORD SWINGER OR A FOOT WASHER?

Insight for the Heart

How long has it been since you put up your sword and picked up a towel? God's kingdom is built with servants. Begin to wipe the debris from your brother's feet. If He did it, we should do it! Practice servanthood. Remember the symbol of His Kingdom is a towel. Peter picked up a sword but was reluctant to embrace the towel. When we pick up our swords instead of towels, Jesus often has to repair the damage done to the Body. The time for indiscriminate sword swinging is over. It's towel time! Put up your sword—pick up your towel! (*God's Dream Team*, p. 74.)

Applications for Life

1. Honestly, what was your answer to the question at the top of this page?

2. If the call to take up a towel disturbs you, consider the fact that you are following the example of Jesus Himself. Now describe where towel ministry will take you.

_____

_____

_____

_____

_____

_____

_____

_____

_____

_____

_____

_____

_____

_____

_____

_____

_____

_____

_____

_____

_____

_____

_____

_____

_____

_____

_____

_____

_____

THE DREAMKEEPER'S PRAYER FOCUS, PART 3

Grant me, and grant us, the grace to walk in humility,
considering others better than ourselves.
May we look after the interests of others
as carefully as we look after our own.
Above all, may my attitude be the same as Yours—
that of a humble servant.

THE CHALLENGE TO CHANGE FROM A PLACE OF STRIFE TO A PLACE OF SAFETY

Insight for the Heart

My aim is to challenge you to change. I want to cause you to think about some things in ways you haven't thought about them before. God has a dream for His Church; He has a dream for every local church. He has a vision for your church. Part of His dream is that it would be "one." He wants us to put our best foot forward so the world can see that we are unified, that there are no divisions or strife. It is time to stop shining our own shoes and become servants to the world. When they look at your church they should say, *This is a place of safety; I can run here and escape the madness everywhere else.* (*God's Dream Team*, p. 75.)

Applications for Life

1. How much time do you spend tending to your own needs and wants, and how much time do you invest in others? Is it a 90/10 split, 80/20, 50/50 or 98/2?

2. What ratio do you think God wants it to be?

3. Are you prepared to say yes?

_____

_____

_____

_____

_____

Grant me, and grant us, the grace to walk in humility,
considering others better than ourselves.
May we look after the interests of others
as carefully as we look after our own.
Above all, may my attitude be the same as Yours—
that of a humble servant.

FORGET THE GOLD AND GLORY—PASS OUT THE TOWELS!

Insight for the Heart

The only way to create that kind of atmosphere, to create that kind of unity, is when the spirit of a servant is birthed. Somebody has to say, I don't care whether any gold or glory goes to anybody, I just want to get a job done. Put up the swords and pass out the towels! *There's no room in the Church for spirits of competition or division, but there is still a lot of room for servants.* (*God's Dream Team*, p. 75.)

Applications for Life

1. How were you trained at home, in school and in your life experiences? To compete for first place at any cost? To "divide and conquer" your enemies and competitors?

2. Did anyone ever mention to you the servant's towel method of advancement and accomplishment before now?

3. Which method is right? (And what will you do about it?)

_____

_____

_____

_____

_____

_____

_____

THE DREAMKEEPER'S PRAYER FOCUS, PART 3

Grant me, and grant us, the grace to walk in humility,
considering others better than ourselves.
May we look after the interests of others
as carefully as we look after our own.
Above all, may my attitude be the same as Yours—
that of a humble servant.

THE FIVE LEVELS OF UNITY

Unity does not just happen. It is not some overnight sensation of the Spirit. Unity is something that builds and grows until it reaches beyond itself.

Is it so hard to comprehend that the God who wrote "precept upon precept, line upon line"[1] would have a divine design for building marriages, friendships, families, communities and the countless local churches that comprise His one Church, His Dream Team? God's design incorporates many levels of unity, and each level of unity yields its own corresponding power to change and affect everything and everyone around it.

The collective power of unity increases with each level. I am going to share with you five levels of unity, although perhaps there are more. Remember and understand that the amount of divine power available on one level rises exponentially as you proceed to the next level.

If you find a crack in a wall, you could plaster it up and it would look good for a while—at least until the next time the weather changes or the ground gets wet. Then that crack would reappear, looking worse than it did before you covered it up.

The only way to really fix a crack that appears on a wall or ceiling is to repair the underlying cause. Once you repair the foundation, you can put plaster over the crack and it will be fine. This same principle applies any time there is a problem in any area of your life. It is the only way to restore broken unity in your spirit, in your family, among your friends or within your local church.

Here's an example. A pastor cannot expect to fix the problem of disunity simply by standing up and preaching a sermon on unity. That is like putting plaster over the crack. If he is a wise pastor, he will instead go to the various groups and family units within the church and ask, "What is the problem? How can we fix this?" He will work among them to get the foundation right. Then he can get up on a Sunday and preach a sermon on unity and the plaster will stick.

If disunity exists in a church, any preaching about unity is generally powerless to fix it. You must trace the disunity to its source, identify the small group where the division originates and deal with it at that level. You cannot repair disunity at the surface level where you see it; you must go underneath and fix it at the foundation. Once you repair the foundation, it will hold.

The same thing is true in marriage. If you and your spouse are having problems, the first thing you should ask yourself is not, *What's wrong with my marriage?* That is putting plaster over the crack. The first thing you need to ask yourself is, *What is wrong with me?* If you fix what is wrong with you, you have repaired your personal foundation. Then you can start working on the marriage, which involves a higher and more complex level of unity between yourself and your spouse.

Now continue your journey to unity with divinity as we walk together brick by brick, level by level, until we become the answer to God's most passionate prayer.

Note
1. Isa. 28:10,13.

INDIVIDUAL UNITY

DOUBLE-MINDEDNESS IS DISUNITY OF THE HEART

Insight for the Heart

The first level of unity in God's kingdom is found within your own self. Do you know that it is possible to have disunity in your own heart? James the apostle was referring to flawed *individual unity* when he said, "A double-minded man is unstable in all his ways."[1] If you can't trust yourself, you are inherently unstable. Stop and think about that. Do you wonder why some people do such illogical or thoughtless things? No one else can trust them because they can't trust themselves! You never know which side they are going to come down on.

Think of a double-minded man about to marry. Shouldn't someone warn that sweet little woman that she is about to marry a double-minded man? This man's internal disunity may cause him to wake up in love with somebody else the next day. It happens. Why?

Double-mindedness. (*God's Dream Team*, p. 78.)

Applications for Life

1. List some areas where you have seen double-mindedness destabilize the lives, relationships and endeavors of people around you.

2. Some people seem to make double-mindedness their personal anthem in life; but all of us battle this problem in some way or another. Are you willing to accept what the Holy Spirit reveals about double-mindedness in your life?

Note
1. Jas. 1:8, *KJV*.

_____
_____
_____
_____
_____
_____
_____
_____
_____
_____
_____
_____
_____
_____
_____
_____
_____
_____
_____
_____
_____
_____
_____

THE DREAMKEEPER'S PRAYER FOCUS, PART 4

Father, forgive me for my selfish motives and my envy of others.
Lord Jesus, let my heart be broken like Your heart,
and may I humble myself to serve others
as faithfully as You served us in Your life, death and resurrection;
let there be no division between me and my brethren.

FIRST THINGS FIRST: DO YOU KNOW WHO YOU ARE?

Insight for the Heart

You can't go to the next level of unity until you have first settled things at a lower level of unity. It would be like trying to build a house without first pouring a foundation. A man doesn't have any business getting married and possibly ruining somebody else's life until he first finds out who *he* is and what *he* is called to do—until he makes his "calling and election sure."[1] One should be able to say "I know who I am. I know in whom I believe. I have an understanding of where I stand in Christ."

There is something to be said about somebody who changes careers as often as some people change shoes, who never knows what he wants to do or who he is. With these types of people you never know whether they are in the church or out of the church. They have slid in and out so much they have worn slick a spot—the proverbial backslider. You have to check on them:

"How are you doing? How are you this week?"

"I'm okay right now. I don't know about next week."

What is the problem? Double-mindedness is the disease; noncommitment is the symptom. (*God's Dream Team*, pp. 78, 79.)

Applications for Life

1. Have you ever been tempted to skip "first grade" and jump ahead to "graduation" in some area of your life (for example, learning a new task at work or moving to a new level of spiritual growth or ministry offering more visibility or responsibility)?

2. In your experience, what happens to people who skip the fundamentals or fail to lay a solid foundation before trying to build higher?

3. How do this disease and its symptoms apply to your life?

Note
1. 2 Pet. 1:10, *NIV.*

THE DREAMKEEPER'S PRAYER FOCUS, PART 4

Father, forgive me for my selfish motives and my envy of others.
Lord Jesus, let my heart be broken like Your heart,
and may I humble myself to serve others
as faithfully as You served us in Your life, death and resurrection;
let there be no division between me and my brethren.

NONE OF THESE THINGS MOVE ME—HOW ABOUT YOU?

Insight for the Heart

The Bible says, "If therefore thine eye be single, thy whole body shall be full of light."[1]

There is something powerful about the single-mindedness of Paul: "This one thing I do."[2] Paul was singular in his focus. We yearn to be able to say, "I am secure in Christ. I am secure in what He has called me to do. I have focus and single-mindedness. I know who I am and where I am going."

If you can find a person who is totally sold out to Christ—a man or woman who knows what he or she is doing, yet does not care if anyone else likes it as long as it pleases Christ—that person is like the apostle who, after giving a long list of possibilities, said, "None of these things move me."[3] That is the ultimate stability. (*God's Dream Team*, p. 79.)

Applications for Life

1. Can you say, "This one thing I do"? Why or why not?

2. Would you like to know who you are and where you are going? Do you know where to start this process?

Notes
1. Matt. 6:22, *KJV*.
2. Phil. 3:13, *NRSV*.
3. Acts 20:24.

_____

_____

_____

_____

_____

_____

_____

_____

_____

_____

_____

_____

_____

_____

_____

_____

_____

_____

_____

_____

_____

_____

_____

_____

_____

_____

THE DREAMKEEPER'S PRAYER FOCUS, PART 4

Father, forgive me for my selfish motives and my envy of others.
Lord Jesus, let my heart be broken like Your heart,
and may I humble myself to serve others
as faithfully as You served us in Your life, death and resurrection;
let there be no division between me and my brethren.

TAP THE POWER OF SINGLE-MINDED FOCUS

Insight for the Heart

What are you moved by? Is it the fear of man that moves you? You would be surprised if you knew the number of ministers who primarily see themselves as ministers to man. The only house God said He would ever rebuild was the Tabernacle of David. That was where the worshipers became the only veil between Jehovah God and the world. They turned their backs on the nation—on man, so to speak—faced the ark and worshiped God. We must understand that our primary calling is to be a minister to Him. Sometimes, in order to see His face, we must turn our backs on man's face. A good conductor knows he must turn his back on the audience to face the music. If you become a minister to Him, whatever flows out of that is fine. It will set us free from the fear of man and make us realize our bondage to the fear of God. There is power in a single-minded focus. (*God's Dream Team*, pp. 79, 80.)

Applications for Life

1. The fear of man and public opinion may be the greatest hindrance to unity in your life and in the Body of Christ. Can you pinpoint and openly confess areas where you are more afraid of men (or women) than of God?

2. Isn't it time to turn your back on the judgmental glances and whispered murmurings of fickle men and seek the face of God? Ask Him to show you where and how to do this and write down what He says to your heart.

_____

_____

_____

_____

_____

_____

_____

_____

_____

_____

_____

_____

_____

_____

_____

_____

_____

_____

_____

_____

_____

_____

_____

THE DREAMKEEPER'S PRAYER FOCUS, PART 4

Father, forgive me for my selfish motives and my envy of others.
Lord Jesus, let my heart be broken like Your heart,
and may I humble myself to serve others
as faithfully as You served us in Your life, death and resurrection;
let there be no division between me and my brethren.

BEWARE THE DANGERS OF SPIRITUAL SCHIZOPHRENIA

Insight for the Heart

I am not going to worry so much about some of the things other parents are concerned about when it is time for my daughters to find spouses. My first priority is to learn if these potential husbands "know who they are." Are their eyes "single"? Do they have spiritual and mental stability? Have they made their "calling and election sure"? Have they focused on who they are both spiritually and secularly?

I don't care if a man washes cars. If that is what he is called to do, is he being the best car washer he can be? He might end up owning 10 car washes! What matters is that he be focused and not double-minded. If he is double-minded, the world would say he has a split personality. (Some people aren't split; they are just slightly cracked and on their way!) Double-mindedness is a form of spiritual schizophrenia. (*God's Dream Team*, p. 80.)

Applications for Life

1. Even the non-Christian world recognizes the dysfunction and danger of having a split personality. Spiritual and mental stability begin with having eyes that are "single." What does this term mean to you?

2. Are you keeping your eyes on the One who is most important in every area of life? Do you have a single focus or a many-splintered approach to life? It could mean the difference between spiritual health and spiritual schizophrenia.

| THE DREAMKEEPER'S PRAYER FOCUS, PART 4 |

Father, forgive me for my selfish motives and my envy of others.
Lord Jesus, let my heart be broken like Your heart,
and may I humble myself to serve others
as faithfully as You served us in Your life, death and resurrection;
let there be no division between me and my brethren.

DEVELOP A SERVANT MENTALITY TOWARD YOUR DESTINY AND PURPOSE

Insight for the Heart

Jesus said He didn't come to speak His own words but to say what He heard His Father say. He didn't come to do His own works but only to do what He saw His Father do. Don't you wish the same could be said of all the preachers and workers in the Church?

Too many times we see Christians pursuing *their* ideas of their eternal destiny and purpose. By definition, these things can only come from God. Let us, as servants in the service of the King, adopt this truth from God's Word and make it our prayer and confession: *Father, my life is not my own, for I have been bought with a price and purchased by the blood of Another. My life and my body are Yours, and I lay down my plans and personal agendas to make room for Your cross in my life. Be glorified in my servanthood and my obedience to Your heavenly vision.*[1] This is how you can develop a Christlike servant mentality toward your own destiny and purpose.

Applications for Life

1. Is it difficult for you to see yourself as a servant? You have no choice because it is the pattern Jesus modeled for us. What areas of your Christian life will have to be remodeled to match the Lord's example?

2. In what ways does a servant respond differently from someone who is not a servant?

Note
1. See 1 Cor. 6:20; 7:23.

_____

_____

_____

_____

_____

_____

_____

_____

_____

_____

_____

_____

_____

_____

_____

_____

_____

_____

_____

_____

_____

_____

_____

_____

_____

THE DREAMKEEPER'S PRAYER FOCUS, PART 4

Father, forgive me for my selfish motives and my envy of others.
Lord Jesus, let my heart be broken like Your heart,
and may I humble myself to serve others
as faithfully as You served us in Your life, death and resurrection;
let there be no division between me and my brethren.

ARE YOU PERSUADED OR IS YOUR FAITH PAPER-THIN?

Insight for the Heart

Paul boldly declared, "I am not ashamed, for I know whom I have believed and am persuaded that He is able to keep what I have committed to Him until that Day."[1] This great apostle exhibited an unshakable confidence in God that carried him through constant dangers, shipwreck, torture and hardships during his ministry.

Do you *know* in whom you have believed? Is Jesus Christ simply the paper-thin Sunday School character hanging on your refrigerator with a magnet, or is He the living Son of God with whom you walk and talk every day? Are you *persuaded* that He is able?

Don't wait until you are surrounded by the darkness of a midnight situation to settle this matter. Do it now, in the bright light of day. That way you will pass the test, whether you find yourself preaching Christ to hostile bikers or locked in a jail at midnight with the wounds of persecution on your back. This is the ultimate test of individual unity.

Applications for Life

1. It is difficult to have faith in someone you hardly know. Do you know in whom you have believed? How do you know you know Him?

2. Have you faced an ultimate test yet? Do you think you are ready for another?

Note
1. 2 Tim. 1:12.

| THE DREAMKEEPER'S PRAYER FOCUS, PART 4 |

Father, forgive me for my selfish motives and my envy of others.
Lord Jesus, let my heart be broken like Your heart,
and may I humble myself to serve others
as faithfully as You served us in Your life, death and resurrection;
let there be no division between me and my brethren.

FAMILY UNITY

FAMILY UNITY BEGINS WITH INDIVIDUAL UNITY

Insight for the Heart

The second level of unity is *family unity*. If you are going to have unity within your family, you must first have individual unity. We can preach and teach "husbands, love your wives,"[1] but until the individual husband and the individual wife find individual unity, there can be no true family unity. Yet if you are going to do what God has called you to do, you must be unified within your family. (*God's Dream Team*, pp. 80, 81.)

Don't fall into the trap of arguing over who is "boss" in the family. Let God's Word be your guide and especially focus on God's command, "Be kindly affectionate to one another with brotherly love, in honor giving preference to one another."[2]

Applications for Life

1. How would you describe your family—unified, somewhat unified or nearly disintegrated? Have you set goals to increase unity in your home?

2. Describe some practical ways you can (and will) show preference toward your spouse or other members of your family today.

Notes
1. Col. 3:19.
2. Rom. 12:10.

| THE DREAMKEEPER'S PRAYER FOCUS, PART 5 |

I pray that my kingdom would go
so that Your kingdom may come.
May my will be broken
so that Your will may be done
on earth as it is in heaven.

PARENTS: WHAT IS THE BEST "GIVEN" YOU'VE GIVEN TO YOUR FAMILY?

Insight for the Heart

I don't remember ever hearing my mom and dad say a cross word to each other while I was growing up. I understand that there were some words said, but the exchanges never happened in front of me or my sister. I am the product of a family filled with unity. What that gives to children is of immeasurable value. They have at least one less worry. I don't have to worry about my family—I know that they love me and they are going to be there for me. That ought to be a "given" in people's lives. (*God's Dream Team*, p. 81.)

Applications for Life

1. Would you say the given state of affairs in your home is peace and respect or strife and disrespect?

2. What do you want to see change over the next few weeks and months?

_____

_____

_____

_____

_____

_____

_____

_____

_____

_____

_____

_____

_____

_____

_____

_____

_____

_____

_____

_____

_____

_____

_____

_____

_____

_____

_____

_____

_____

_____

_____

_____

THE DREAMKEEPER'S PRAYER FOCUS, PART 5

I pray that my kingdom would go
so that Your kingdom may come.
May my will be broken
so that Your will may be done
on earth as it is in heaven.

MY DADDY LOVES ME

Insight for the Heart

One of the first full sentences that I taught all three of my daughters when they were still in their cribs began with a question: *What are you supposed to always remember?*

There were hardly two days that would go by without my asking them. The answer that I taught them by rote was *My Daddy loves me.*

When they learned that much, the lesson/game expanded:

"When does he love you?"

"All the time."

"Does he love you when you're good?"

"Yes!"

"Does he love you when you're bad?"

"Yes!"

Do you recognize what I am teaching them? I am placing in their foundations something that is so stable, they will never have to worry about it: I am their father, I love them unconditionally and I am never going to leave them. (*God's Dream Team*, pp. 81, 82.)

Applications for Life

1. Can you remember those times when you knew you failed your parents, your spouse or other family members? Did you fail to remember what you are always supposed to remember, or did that even apply in your family situation?

2. Why is unconditional love so important to the health of families? Can you think of examples from your life or others' lives that support your answer?

3. What kind of love do you extend to the members of your family?

_____

_____

_____

_____

_____

_____

_____

_____

_____

_____

_____

_____

_____

_____

_____

_____

_____

_____

_____

_____

_____

_____

| THE DREAMKEEPER'S PRAYER FOCUS, PART 5 |

*I pray that my kingdom would go
so that Your kingdom may come.
May my will be broken
so that Your will may be done
on earth as it is in heaven.*

DON'T WORRY: I'M ON YOUR SIDE (EVEN THOUGH YOU FAIL)

Insight for the Heart

Another Father said one time, "Little children, these things write I unto you, that ye sin not. And if any man sin, we have an advocate with the Father."[1] Jesus will argue for our forgiveness. In other words, the Lord is telling us, "You don't have to worry about Me; I'm on your side." (*God's Dream Team*, p. 83.)

The biblical pattern seems to establish the man of the house as the ultimate authority or disciplinarian and the woman of the house as the primary nurturer. Obviously, this is a very soft line that varies greatly with the personalities, gifts and responsibilities of the individuals in each marriage. However, God holds men particularly responsible for the behavior and overall direction of their homes. At times, compassionate wives and mothers will intercede with their husbands on behalf of children who have done something worthy of punishment or correction. This is neither wrong nor indicative of sentimental weakness. We see this pattern in the relationship of Jesus and His Father.

The Father obviously knows all things, including the value and necessity of mercy and grace toward His very flawed earthly children. Yet He has ordained that the Son intercede for us continually.

In this divine paradigm, we see the love of God continually displayed in Jesus' passionate prayers on our behalf; and we also see God's love and mercy displayed in the way our heavenly Father graciously grants the prayers and petitions of His Son on our behalf.

This gentle dynamic of righteousness balanced with grace is a pattern we should follow in our own homes. It will bring peace, joy and heavenly unity—even in the midst of our wholly apparent humanity.

Note
1. 1 John 2:1, *KJV*.

Applications for Life

1. Why did Jesus describe His relationship with His Father in terms of family relationships? Was it an accident or a divine directive and explicit example for our relationships on earth?

2. Is there anything about Jesus' relationship to His Father that triggers a longing in your heart for something that is missing in your life? (If so, describe it. If not, can you explain why?)

_____

_____

_____

_____

_____

_____

_____

_____

_____

_____

_____

_____

_____

_____

_____

THE DREAMKEEPER'S PRAYER FOCUS, PART 5

I pray that my kingdom would go
so that Your kingdom may come.
May my will be broken
so that Your will may be done
on earth as it is in heaven.

WILL THE SEEDS YOU SOW WITH YOUR TONGUE MAKE YOUR CHILDREN BETTER OR BITTER?

Insight for the Heart

Another thing I can honestly report about my upbringing is that no matter how tough the circumstances were in the work of the Kingdom, I never heard either my father or mother speak badly of anyone. This sowed the seeds in my own life that enabled me to grow better instead of bitter.

Very often when we allow unity to be destroyed on one level—for instance, in the local church—we are surprised when it affects the unity on another level. (*God's Dream Team*, pp. 83, 84.)

Well-intentioned but misguided people who sow discord in their local churches only reap that discord in their own lives and the lives of their children.

As I noted earlier, these levels of unity are so intricately interconnected that when you pull one thread out of its proper place, it will often unravel a large part of the garment. (*God's Dream Team*, p. 84.)

Applications for Life

1. The Bible makes it clear that the tongue is more difficult to control than any other member of our bodies. Perhaps the biggest problem is that too few of us even *attempt* to control our tongues, and when we do, we don't seek His help in the trying. Do you?

2. Did the example set by your parents help you to become better or bitter? What has *your* example done in the lives of those you love?

_____

_____

_____

_____

_____

_____

_____

_____

_____

_____

_____

_____

_____

_____

_____

_____

_____

_____

_____

_____

_____

_____

_____

THE DREAMKEEPER'S PRAYER FOCUS, PART 5

I pray that my kingdom would go
so that Your kingdom may come.
May my will be broken
so that Your will may be done
on earth as it is in heaven.

WHAT DOES IT MEAN TO HAVE YOUR FAMILY "IN ORDER"?

Insight for the Heart

According to Scripture, a man is not supposed to be a bishop (overseer) unless he has his family in order.[1] I think this may possibly be as much an observation as a commandment. *If a man does not have the ability to create and maintain unity within his family, you can put him in the position of a pastor, but he won't be successful at that higher level.* These levels of unity build one upon another. (*God's Dream Team*, p. 84.)

The key phrase in this discussion is "family in order." We need to learn how God defines order and then conform to His way instead of ours. A legalist would have dismissed the ministry of Billy Graham during the season when his son rebelled and withdrew into the world; but God didn't seem to take that view. And there are hundreds of thousands and perhaps millions of Christians today who are eternally thankful for God's grace toward Dr. Graham!

The Grahams raised their son in the best way they could in a Christ-centered home. Yet when their son entered adulthood, he made a clear choice to run from what was right. Today, that prodigal son is an anointed and dedicated minister of the gospel who is assuming the leadership role in the ministry established many decades ago by his father.

There is a vast difference between children who rebel *because* of their parents' ungodly and nonbiblical methods of parenting and discipline—epitomized by the lax fathering of Eli the priest in the Old Testament[2]—and children who are strong-willed in adolescence and/or adulthood and temporarily rebel from the *right teachings* of their parents. Many of the greatest leaders in the Church were rebellious or difficult children who were raised by godly parents.

All of this is bound up with God's sovereign decision to give us free choice. Our children must eventually choose for themselves whom they will serve. Our part is to diligently teach, train and disciple them in the truth of God's Word and the nurture of His glorious presence. My conviction is that once our children "taste and see that the LORD is good,"[3] they will never be happy drinking from any other source.

Applications for Life

1. Did you grow up in a godly home without any sojourns into rebellion, or were you a temporary prodigal before coming to Christ?

2. If you are or have been a parent, how does your parenting scorecard look? What changes might produce more godly order in your home?

Notes
1. See 1 Tim. 3:2-5, *NIV*.
2. See 1 Sam. 2:22-32.
3. Ps. 34:8.

THE DREAMKEEPER'S PRAYER FOCUS, PART 5

*I pray that my kingdom would go
so that Your kingdom may come.
May my will be broken
so that Your will may be done
on earth as it is in heaven.*

BIBLICAL SUBMISSION AND CHAUVINISTIC ATTITUDES CANNOT COEXIST IN A MARRIAGE

Insight for the Heart

The familiar analogy that God took woman from man's side to walk beside him and not behind him is true to God's original intent. This truth should remove any chauvinistic attitudes men entertain about ruling as masters over women. A truly biblical marriage involves two people who have mutually submitted to one another's divine destiny in Christ. Divorce is often born of the disease of disunity and the familiar issue of control. It strikes at the most basic building block of the home. We should never seek to put anybody "under" us—even (or especially) our spouses. Our goal should be to put ourselves under the authority of Christ and urge others to do likewise.

When we learn to *empower* instead of *overpower*, we weave again the "basket of unity" that is God's ordained "container" for the happiness of the family unit. (*God's Dream Team*, pp. 84, 85.)

Application for Life

1. The only way you can be submitted to a spouse's divine destiny is if you actually believe he or she *has* one. If you are married, describe what you believe is the divine destiny of your spouse and how you support that destiny. (If you are single, describe the divine destiny of a family member or friend and how you are empowering that person to pursue it.)

| THE DREAMKEEPER'S PRAYER FOCUS, PART 5 |

I pray that my kingdom would go
so that Your kingdom may come.
May my will be broken
so that Your will may be done
on earth as it is in heaven.

UNITY IN THE COMMUNITY

GOOD FRIENDS TEND TO HAVE OLD FRIENDS

Insight for the Heart

We have already examined the first two levels of unity, *individual* unity and *family* unity. Now we look at the third level of unity, the unity of *community*—your friends.

One of the first things I want to know about someone if I am going to work with that person closely is whether he or she has kept and maintained close relationships with some friends for a long time. Wisdom warns us: *Never trust anybody who cannot maintain long-term friendships.*

You can't stay close to every old friend; but you can stay close to *some* old friends. If friends can't get along with an individual, what makes me think I am going to be able to get along with that person? If every one of a person's best friendships only last for six months, there's a relationship problem. (*God's Dream Team*, p. 85.)

Applications for Life

1. According to the friendship equation above, are you a trustworthy candidate for long-term friendship or are you mostly a short-term friend?

2. List the two or three people closest to you who are not part of your family. Then describe their personalities. Are they like you or are they closer to being your opposite? How do you get along with them?

_____

_____

_____

_____

_____

_____

_____

_____

_____

_____

_____

_____

_____

_____

_____

_____

_____

_____

_____

_____

_____

_____

THE DREAMKEEPER'S PRAYER FOCUS, PART 6

Lord, cause me to be single-minded
and sure of Your calling upon my life.
May unity of heart and mind prevail in my home,
in my community of friends and family,
in my local church and in the Church around the world
as we focus upon You, our risen Lord, Master, King and Savior.

BE FRIENDS WITH A FEW AND BE FRIENDLY WITH EVERYONE ELSE

Insight for the Heart

When a person has "old friends" in his life, it tells me that this person has learned to keep peace, has forgiven wrongs, has been forgiven and has accepted differences. This person learned both the value and the price of commitment. If you are having problems maintaining long-term friendships, you ought to check your foundations, the lower levels of unity. All of these things are interlaced, one layer on top of another.

I refer to this third level as *koinonia*—unity among our friends. Koinonia is a Greek word meaning, basically, "community"—love and commitment among friends. This could also be cell groups, Sunday School classes or any natural grouping of people. The foundation of strength in the local church is here. I have heard preachers preach against cliques. That is foolishness. You cannot be best friends with everybody. There are going to be people with whom you feel a natural kinship. Be friends with them and be friendly with everyone else. (*God's Dream Team*, pp. 85, 86.)

Applications for Life

1. How are the foundations of your friendships? Do you find yourself criticizing your friends regularly or do you speak honestly while offering them unconditional love?

2. Do you agree that koinonia, or the community of friends, is a foundation of strength for the Church? Why?

THE DREAMKEEPER'S PRAYER FOCUS, PART 6

Lord, cause me to be single-minded
and sure of Your calling upon my life.
May unity of heart and mind prevail in my home,
in my community of friends and family,
in my local church and in the Church around the world
as we focus upon You, our risen Lord, Master, King and Savior.

THE CULTIVATION OF FRIENDSHIPS CREATES UNITY AND BUILDS THE CHURCH

Insight for the Heart

It is necessary that there be tight-knit groups giving mutual support in the Body of Christ. The Church is made out of stones, not individual grains of sand. So cultivate friendships. Some churches facilitate this through cell groups; others rely on Sunday School classes and other activities to foster friendships. However it is done, it must be done. Friends, peers, buddies, pals or gals, fellow cowboys, dudes from the 'hood—groups are an integral part of creating unity and building the Church. (*God's Dream Team*, p. 87.)

We should all meet new people and make new friends, but it is healthy to cultivate and maintain deep, long-term friendships. One side benefit to multiyear, deep, trusting friendships is that when your children can't talk to you, they know they can talk to *those* friends. You trust them and your family knows you trust them. (*God's Dream Team*, p. 86.)

I think God has planned from eternity for each of us to enjoy these extended family relationships where commonly held values and life goals are constantly reinforced and reaffirmed by other voices outside of relationships in the home.

Applications for Life

1. It is healthy for Christians to have friends outside of their local church as well as within; but the most vital relationships should be those whose bonds go deeper than koinonia. The blood bonds between born-again Christian friends is able to carry them through the worst trials and temptations life can bring because they are rooted in both the human soul and the Spirit of Christ. Who are the blood brothers and blood sisters among your closest friends?

2. The Bible says there is a "friend who sticks closer than a brother."[1] Would you *really* consider Jesus to be this kind of friend?

Note

1. Prov. 18:24.

_____

_____

_____

_____

_____

_____

_____

_____

_____

_____

_____

_____

_____

_____

_____

_____

| THE DREAMKEEPER'S PRAYER FOCUS, PART 6 |

Lord, cause me to be single-minded
and sure of Your calling upon my life.
May unity of heart and mind prevail in my home,
in my community of friends and family,
in my local church and in the Church around the world
as we focus upon You, our risen Lord, Master, King and Savior.

WE HAVE LAUGHED TOGETHER UNTIL OUR THROATS ACHED

by Bishop Joseph L. Garlington
Senior Pastor, Covenant Church of Pittsburgh
Pittsburgh, Pennsylvania

I have asked some friends both old and new to join me in addressing the friendship components of unity. Joseph Garlington's skin is a different color from mine, but his heart beats in syncopation with my heart. We are truly "blood brothers" in Christ. I love him dearly.

Insight for the Heart

I believe genuine friendships are birthed in the Spirit. "Whatever is born of God overcomes."[1] From the first time I met Tommy, he was hungry for God. I had just come from a conference in Toronto and had been powerfully touched by God. I didn't say a lot about it, but Tommy sensed it. We prayed together, and the Holy Spirit knitted our hearts together in that moment.

If we haven't seen each other for a few days or weeks, it only takes a simple phone call to refresh the friendship, and we continue as though we have been together every day. We can talk about anything, and we are possessive about nothing. Our ministry times together are a reflection, first of all, of our friendship with the Holy Spirit and, secondly, of our friendship with one another. We have wept together in the presence of an awesome God; and in the Cracker Barrel restaurant in Atlanta, we have laughed together until our throats ached.

Applications for Life

1. Do you have a friend with whom you can talk about anything and be possessive about nothing? Describe him or her.

2. Are you that kind of friend to others?

Note
1. 1 John 5:4.

THE DREAMKEEPER'S PRAYER FOCUS, PART 6

Lord, cause me to be single-minded
and sure of Your calling upon my life.
May unity of heart and mind prevail in my home,
in my community of friends and family,
in my local church and in the Church around the world
as we focus upon You, our risen Lord, Master, King and Savior.

THE REWARD OF FRIENDSHIP IS TRUSTING AND BEING TRUSTED

by Pastor Mickey Friend
Apostolic Bible Church
St. Paul, Minnesota

*Mickey Friend is my friend! I have bandaged his heart wounds
(and sometimes those of his children), and he has lovingly applied the balm
of Gilead to me and my family—a true friend!*

Insight for the Heart

A friend loveth at all times—good times and bad. As I have grown older and hopefully wiser, the value of true friendship has been elevated to the highest place in my world. Spending yourself for someone else doesn't always make good business sense. Helping someone else move upward (often at your own expense) doesn't always make good political sense. But the reward of friendship—trusting and being trusted—affords a life-long sense of peace and safety in knowing that you will never be alone. This is the true blessing of a friendship.

Tommy Tenney and I began our friendship as fishing buddies. (Sounds pretty "New Testament," doesn't it?) Some of the funniest and most tragic moments I've known have been shared with him. Our relationship has always been encompassed by ministry and vision for the kingdom of God. This is why my heart rejoices as I see Tom soar on fresh winds of the Spirit, bringing hope, encouragement and healing to the Body of Christ.

Applications for Life

1. Do you agree with Mickey Friend's statement about the reward of friendship? How does your trust level vary between your close friends and those who are just acquaintances?

2. Do you have any really close friends whom you *can't* trust? Are *you* trustworthy?

_____

_____

_____

_____

_____

_____

_____

_____

_____

_____

_____

_____

_____

_____

_____

_____

_____

_____

THE DREAMKEEPER'S PRAYER FOCUS, PART 6

Lord, cause me to be single-minded
and sure of Your calling upon my life.
May unity of heart and mind prevail in my home,
in my community of friends and family,
in my local church and in the Church around the world
as we focus upon You, our risen Lord, Master, King and Savior.

WILL THE FRIENDS YOU'VE CHOSEN MAKE YOU OR BREAK YOU?

by Rev. Charles Green
Faith Church
New Orleans, Louisiana

I selected Charles Green as my pastor; he became my friend.
Hardly a week goes by without us conversing. A generation stands between our ages,
but we don't know it! I have learned to balance my foolishness
with wise friends . . . like Charles.

Insight for the Heart

We are stuck with our relatives, but we can pick our friends. During your lifetime, the kinds of friends you have will powerfully affect your life for good or for evil. In a very real sense, the influence of your friends can help make you or break you.

The Bible declares, "Confidence in an unfaithful man in time of trouble is like a bad tooth and a foot out of joint."[1] God's Word also warns us that unfriendly people do not usually have good friends because "a man who has friends must himself be friendly."[2]

For these reasons, it is true that your survival may depend on the type of friends you have. It is inevitable that there will come a time in your life when you will face an emergency or low place that is too great for you to face alone. Obviously, no one actually sets out to fail or fall into trouble; it just happens. When it does, the Bible's warning always applies: "Woe to him who is *alone when he falls*."[3]

We have the privilege of making the same choice as Abraham, of whom it is said, "He was called the friend of God."[4] We also have the privilege of selecting our friends and cherishing them in the same way that David cherished his friend of the heart, Jonathan.

Applications for Life

1. Do you have the kinds of friends who are willing to suffer with you just as they are willing to rejoice with you? Describe how they demonstrate their friendship.

2. Are you that kind of friend, too? How can you be a better friend than you are now?

Notes
1. Prov. 25:19.
2. Prov. 18:24.
3. Eccles. 4:10, emphasis mine. Also read vv. 9-12.
4. Jas. 2:23.

THE DREAMKEEPER'S PRAYER FOCUS, PART 6

Lord, cause me to be single-minded
and sure of Your calling upon my life.
May unity of heart and mind prevail in my home,
in my community of friends and family,
in my local church and in the Church around the world
as we focus upon You, our risen Lord, Master, King and Savior.

GUARD AND PRESERVE YOUR KINGDOM CONNECTIONS

by Jentezen Franklin
Senior Pastor, Free Chapel Worship Center
Gainesville, Georgia

Jentezen Franklin is my friend. And he is a Jonathan to me.
I don't know how to say it any better than this.

Insight for the Heart

Loneliness is a terrible thing, but aloneness with God is a must. Those who serve in the ministry know that it can be one of the loneliest of occupations. Though you minister to a multitude, there can be a gnawing emptiness that cries out for true friendship with someone to whom you can relate.

From the first time Tommy Tenney and I met, our hearts seemed to be in syncopation with each other. Tommy is what I call a "Kingdom connection"—an eternal friend whom God places in your life. We don't have to work at being friends; the bond is just there. Even though we may go for weeks without seeing or speaking to one another due to our schedules, when we do reconnect, we seem to just pick up right where we left off.

God's Word tells us deep calls unto deep and iron sharpens iron.[1] A man's successes and failures many times can be attributed to the close friends with whom he surrounds himself. I am grateful to have Tommy Tenney in my inner circle; he is a true friend. I pray that God would give every believer such a friend.

Applications for Life

1. Consider the people who belong to your "inner circle" of friends. Would you consider any of them to be what Jentezen Franklin calls Kingdom connections?

2. Why do you think God gives us such friends? Is it merely for our benefit or is there something larger involved?

Note

1. See Ps. 42:7; Prov. 27:17.

_____

_____

_____

_____

_____

_____

_____

_____

_____

_____

_____

_____

_____

_____

_____

_____

_____

_____

_____

| THE DREAMKEEPER'S PRAYER FOCUS, PART 6 |

*Lord, cause me to be single-minded
and sure of Your calling upon my life.
May unity of heart and mind prevail in my home,
in my community of friends and family,
in my local church and in the Church around the world
as we focus upon You, our risen Lord, Master, King and Savior.*

LOCAL
CHURCH
UNITY

YOUR FOCUS WILL BE MY FOCUS AND MY VISION WILL BE YOUR VISION

Insight for the Heart

Now we turn our focus to the fourth level of unity: *local church unity*.

When God pulls together groups of people who are focused and single-minded and share a common understanding about what God has called them to do, you have local church unity. This is why you should only want the people in your local church whom God sends, because their focus will match your focus. You will all have similar visions that interlace one with another, so you won't be trying to force a round peg into a square hole all the time. Yes, there are other visions for other things, but other people can do that work if you are not called to do it or commanded to do it by God's Word. Find where your vision leads and follow it. (*God's Dream Team*, pp. 87, 88.)

Applications for Life

1. Have you noticed that some churches just seem to flow toward a common goal with great ease and productivity, while others can barely agree where to mount a coat rack? Describe what you perceive about these congregations.

2. Are you in agreement with the focus and vision of your local church? Why or why not? What are you going to do about it?

_____

_____

_____

_____

_____

_____

_____

_____

_____

_____

_____

_____

_____

_____

_____

_____

_____

_____

_____

_____

| THE DREAMKEEPER'S PRAYER FOCUS, PART 7 |

Break down the barriers that separate us,
and bind Your people together again in Your love.
Raise up those among us who have fallen.
Cause Your compassion to stir our hearts
and impregnate us with Your purposes.
May our chief loyalty be to You and to everyone
who shares our common bloodline in the Lamb who was slain.

GOD MAKES HIS CHILDREN "CLIQUE" FOR SPECIALIZED PURPOSES

Insight for the Heart

The building blocks of unity are homogeneous units—family and like-minded people—who comprise a church body. As I stated, we often hear preaching and negative comments against the natural cliques in our churches. Considering the negative aspects of the exclusive behavior of some of these units, this criticism may be partially right. However, it is the cohesiveness of groups of people with shared interests and shared lifestyles that build koinonia. Local church unity springs from koinonia. (*God's Dream Team*, p. 88.)

If God's work in the created world is any indication, He is the One behind some of these "units" of individuals. As I understand it, even though each cell in the human body shares a common DNA "fingerprint," certain cells are grouped together and modified in the body for highly specialized functions. These "cliques" of like-gifted cells form such vital organs as the kidneys, the liver, the lungs, the spleen and, of course, the human heart.

Very often our heavenly Father binds our hearts and souls to other members of His earthly Body who have the same commitment to evangelism or children's ministry or discipleship training or missions outreach. We all care about these areas of church life and ministry, but most of us tend to gravitate naturally toward one or two specialized areas in which we excel by God's grace and design.

Applications for Life

1. What cliques do you belong to in your local church and why?

2. How might shared likes, dislikes and abilities be part of a great plan orchestrated by God?

_____
_____
_____
_____
_____
_____
_____
_____
_____
_____
_____
_____
_____
_____
_____
_____
_____
_____
_____
_____
_____

THE DREAMKEEPER'S PRAYER FOCUS, PART 7

Break down the barriers that separate us,
and bind Your people together again in Your love.
Raise up those among us who have fallen.
Cause Your compassion to stir our hearts
and impregnate us with Your purposes.
May our chief loyalty be to You and to everyone
who shares our common bloodline in the Lamb who was slain.

IT'S TIME FOR UNITY IN THE CHURCH, NOT DIVISION IN THE "DIVINE DAYCARE"

Insight for the Heart

The epistles of Paul, Peter and John were generally addressed "to the church of God which is at Corinth"[1] or "to the church of the Thessalonians"[2] or to "the church of the Laodiceans"[3] or to one of the other early city churches. In the New Testament era, it was inconceivable for one group of Christians in a city to call or consider themselves a church totally distinct from any other group in that city.

I have a feeling it is still inconceivable to God. Each time He tries to speak to the undershepherds overseeing His Church in a city, He must feel like He has walked into a Kingdom daycare center filled with possessive three-year-olds all trying to protect "their stuff" from the others (even though it all belongs to Daddy). It is time for unity to come to the divine daycare, to fulfill our destiny as the one blood-bought Church under Christ.

More and more of us are beginning to understand how our Father feels. We all sense that the time has come for us to drop our stuff and run to Daddy with one heart and one mind. When we finally release our grip on our "exclusive insights into Heaven" and begin to share our common love for God, we will have answered Jesus' most passionate prayer.

On a more practical level, the only way the church (singular) in your city can accomplish the will of God is for the various parts of the local family to gather around Christ and lift Him up *together*. They may be surprised to find that He may suddenly appear in their midst just to witness and experience the rare miracle of unity.

Notes
1. 2 Cor. 1:1.
2. 1 Thess. 1:1.
3. Rev. 3:14.

Applications for Life

1. Does your local church function on the "Us Four and No More" plan, or does it function as if it were only a small part of a much larger Church? Explain how you know this by describing the outward fruit or evidence of your church's convictions.

2. Are there other churches in your area that show evidence they have caught a glimpse of God's plan, that the Church is larger and greater than their local assembly of believers? What are they doing about it? What are *you* doing about it?

_____

_____

_____

_____

_____

_____

_____

_____

THE DREAMKEEPER'S PRAYER FOCUS, PART 7

Break down the barriers that separate us,
and bind Your people together again in Your love.
Raise up those among us who have fallen.
Cause Your compassion to stir our hearts
and impregnate us with Your purposes.
May our chief loyalty be to You and to everyone
who shares our common bloodline in the Lamb who was slain.

NONE OF US "TASTES RIGHT" ALONE

by T. F. Tenney

My father, T. F. Tenney, has served in the ministry for a half century at this writing. He has influenced hundreds, if not thousands, of pastors, teachers, evangelists and everyday working believers—including me. He always said, "The school of suffering graduates rare scholars." He ought to know. Most of what I know about unity and the Christian life I learned from him. It is a joy to include my father's insights in this journal.

Insight for the Heart

Unity in the Old Testament was taught via five elements. If you enter the door of Exodus 30 and open the pantry of verses 23 through 30, you will find five ingredients there: myrrh, calamus, cassia, cinnamon and oil. Some are bitter; some are sweet. Myrrh was bitter, cinnamon a sweet spice. Calamus was a straight reed, unbending, and cassia was a bark. In the *King James Version*, these are called "principal spices."

The word "principal" is translated from the Hebrew word *roŝh*, which means "head person, chief or leader." Whether or not you are a chief or a leader, you probably know by now that all of us "taste" a little different. However, it was the oil—the anointing—that made all of these spices flow together. *The oil produced unity in their diversity*. None of us would "taste right" alone because each needs the other. It is called Body ministry. Even the head needs the foot, or as Paul said, "that which every joint supplieth."[1]

There was a price of so many shekels on each of the ingredients listed in Exodus 30—except for the oil. There was no price on the olive oil, just an instruction to get "a hin" of it (approximately six quarts).[2] The incense was apparently more oil than anything else, implying that our distinct personalities must be submerged in the oil of the Holy Spirit.

Someone once observed that there may be a price on each of us. I suppose someone could actually determine the worth of our ministry, our abilities, our education and our talents. The oil is another matter—it is priceless. Even in our day, there has to be more of the oil than anything else. The problem is that unity is not an accident; it is made.

Jesus prayed, "That they may be *made* perfect in one."[3] Paul said, "Endeavoring to keep the unity."[4] You have to work at unity, but the rewards are heavenly. "Behold, how good and how pleasant it is."[5]

Applications for Life

1. This illustration centers around the priestly incense reserved for holy purposes. Is there a direct link to the five ministry gifts mentioned in Ephesians 4?

2. How would you go about making unity? When do you plan to start?

Notes
1. Eph. 4:16, *KJV*.
2. Exod. 30:24.
3. John 17:23, *KJV*, emphasis mine.
4. Eph. 4:3.
5. Ps. 133:1.

_____

_____

_____

_____

_____

_____

_____

_____

_____

_____

THE DREAMKEEPER'S PRAYER FOCUS, PART 7

Break down the barriers that separate us,
and bind Your people together again in Your love.
Raise up those among us who have fallen.
Cause Your compassion to stir our hearts
and impregnate us with Your purposes.
May our chief loyalty be to You and to everyone
who shares our common bloodline in the Lamb who was slain.

UNITY COMES WHEN WE ARE SUBMERGED IN THE OIL OF THE HOLY SPIRIT

by T. F. Tenney

Insight for the Heart

God's perfect example of unity is the human body. The body has many parts, but the parts don't all serve the same function. The head is designed to control all the various parts and keep them in unity. The head may say that the left hand doesn't have the anointing to shave but the right hand does. Regardless, the head says to all the parts, "Watch out for and protect the others."

Jealousy is a foreign notion to the physical body (unless you include cancer in the makeup). The right foot is never known to be jealous of the left foot. No, the different parts of the body watch out for one another.

Have you noticed that pain *unifies* the body? I don't care how dirty the foot is, if it gets cut, the foot goes up and the hand comes down to grab it! If the left arm gets broken and is out of action, the right arm doesn't say, "Thank God—one more competitor out of business!" There is no jealousy.

If the right hand gets broken, the rest of the body doesn't say, "You can't shave anymore because you are broken. In fact, you don't deserve to be part of this body ever again!" Nor does the foot say, "I don't want to be a foot anymore. I'm stuck in a shoe all day. Nobody can see me down here. It's hot and it smells. I believe I'll quit and become a hand." And what if my foot then left its assigned place and position? The foot would be out of order, and the body would be a mess!

The foot has a ministry: to tread on scorpions. And the hands have a ministry: to lay hands on the sick. It is time to step into our assigned places: Foot, you stomp the devil. Hands, you heal the sick. Ears, you listen for the voice of God. If you stub your toe, do you vote to see whether you will help it? No, it's involuntary help—that is, *everywhere except in the Church*.

Unity—that's the watchword. Listen to the Head. He will tell you what to do and keep you together.

Applications for Life

1. As you read this selection, what came to your mind? Did you think of things you have said or that you have heard others say?

2. The human body has five appendages—a head, two legs and two arms. Each hand and foot has five digits. How does this imagery apply to your church?

3. What will you do to remove jealousy from your relationships and your service to God in the local church?

| THE DREAMKEEPER'S PRAYER FOCUS, PART 7 |

Break down the barriers that separate us,
and bind Your people together again in Your love.
Raise up those among us who have fallen.
Cause Your compassion to stir our hearts
and impregnate us with Your purposes.
May our chief loyalty be to You and to everyone
who shares our common bloodline in the Lamb who was slain.

EVEN CHURCHES MUST DIE TO SELF·

by Francis Frangipane
Pastor, River of Life Ministries
Cedar Rapids, Iowa

Insight for the Heart[1]

The issues that divide churches are not so much doctrinal as personal.
As leaders, we are too insecure. Jesus said that unless a grain of wheat
falls to the ground and dies, *it abides by itself alone.*[2]

What is true on a personal level is also true on a Churchwide level.
As churches, if we do not die to self, we will abide by ourselves alone. If
we die to self-centeredness, we will bear much fruit. That doesn't mean
we abandon our individual programs or unique congregational con-
cerns but, rather, that our vision and direction are bigger. We must begin
to see the Church from Christ's perspective.

I have to confess that as the pastor of a local church, I have been self-
centered in my service to the Lord. What I mean is that I've wanted *my*
church to be blessed more than other churches. This desire is not pure.

Christ has called me to deny myself and take up my cross daily and
follow Him (actually, He has called you as well).[3] *Now* when God blesses
other churches, I promote them from our pulpit. When special services
are going on elsewhere, we advertise them and encourage our congregation to go. In so doing, the self in me dies, but Christ in me moves forward to ever-increasing freedom.

Application for Life

1. List some other biblical truths that apply on a personal level
   and describe how they also apply at a local-church level. How
   can you apply these truths in practical ways at your church?

Notes

1. Francis Frangipane, "Cedar Rapids Unity," *In Christ's Image* (Internet publication of Arrow Publications, 1999). Used by permission. This and other resources are available at www.frangipane.org.
2. See John 12:24.
3. See Luke 9:23,24.

| THE DREAMKEEPER'S PRAYER FOCUS, PART 7 |

Break down the barriers that separate us,
and bind Your people together again in Your love.
Raise up those among us who have fallen.
Cause Your compassion to stir our hearts
and impregnate us with Your purposes.
May our chief loyalty be to You and to everyone
who shares our common bloodline in the Lamb who was slain.

When Churches Unify, God Commands His Blessing on a City

by Francis Frangipane
Pastor, River of Life Ministries
Cedar Rapids, Iowa

Insight for the Heart

If there is going to be progress in your city, it is because someone is willing to pay the price. That is what the Cross does: Before breakthroughs come, the Cross positions us to pay a price that no one else sees.

I pastor a church in Cedar Rapids, Iowa. Over the last 10 years, pastors and churches across our city have come together in citywide prayer meetings and prayer walks, and we have exchanged pulpits and shared offerings as needed. During one 18-month period, we gathered in the mayor's office to pray for the mayor and city officials who joined us. We believe the statistics show that our prayers led to more than 30 months without a murder in our city! Recently, city churches cooperated in a spirit of unity and led more than 5,000 souls to Christ in one season.

There is a simple, yet profound, effect of possessing loving relationships among pastors in a city. The Lord promised that where the brethren dwell together in unity, there the Lord commands His blessing—life forevermore.[1] We in Cedar Rapids certainly are not perfected yet; however, in very real and tangible ways, we have enjoyed God's commanded blessing as the fruit of unity among our local church bodies.

Where Christ is revealed in His people, heaven accompanies our efforts to turn our cities toward God.

Note
1. See Psalm 133.

Applications for Life

1. Unity begins when God's people deny themselves and take up the Cross. Is there a crease in your shoulder marking the familiar weight of Christ's cross? Or is there a chip of disdain or unforgiveness marking the too familiar point of division between you and certain brethren in your church or city?

_____

_____

_____

_____

_____

_____

_____

_____

_____

_____

_____

_____

_____

THE DREAMKEEPER'S PRAYER FOCUS, PART 7

Break down the barriers that separate us,
and bind Your people together again in Your love.
Raise up those among us who have fallen.
Cause Your compassion to stir our hearts
and impregnate us with Your purposes.
May our chief loyalty be to You and to everyone
who shares our common bloodline in the Lamb who was slain.

UNITY AMONG CHURCHES

AN INWARD FOCUS INDICATES A LOCAL CHURCH MAY BE TREADING WATER WHERE UNITY IS CONCERNED

Insight for the Heart

Have you ever asked yourself why Satan devotes so much energy toward planting seeds of envy, distrust, dissension and pride in our local churches? The enemy knows he is powerless to destroy the Church or to confront the power of God openly; but he also knows that what worked in the Garden of Eden will also work in God's earthly vineyard today.

Think about this: If a church expends all of its energy trying to create and keep unity inside its four walls, the congregation members surely won't have time and energy to go out and promote unity in their city, especially among different local expressions of Christ's Body. It is all they can do to keep their noses above the waterline; they are desperately trying to tread water to survive themselves. (*God's Dream Team*, p. 89.)

All of this speaks of an *inward focus* that all but negates the power of a local church to focus *outward* in obedience to Christ's command: "Go into all the world and preach the gospel to every creature."[1]

The key to solving this problem is to do things God's way, not man's way. It begins and ends with the cross of self-denial and absolute obedience to the will of God, not with unity committees or a seven-week sermon series extolling the value and necessity of unity. **Unity among the churches** begins with unity in individual hearts and proceeds to unity in the home, in a community of friends and in the local church.

Above all, unity is manifested as we take our eyes off one another to worship and gaze with awe, adoration and divine hunger upon the face of the King of glory. The apostle Paul described this miraculous process of transformation to the church at Corinth: "But we all, with unveiled face, beholding as in a mirror the glory of the Lord, are being transformed into the same image from glory to glory, just as by the Spirit of the Lord."[2]

Applications for Life

1. You have probably heard someone say that the best way to overcome the pressure of your own problems is to find others in need and help them with their problems. This is actually a biblical concept that is valid for local churches as well as for our individual lives. Is there an area where you sense your local church has become too inward in its focus?

2. Will you commit yourself to pray for your church family and the church leadership in this area?

Notes
1. Mark 16:15.
2. 2 Cor. 3:18.

_____

_____

_____

_____

_____

_____

_____

_____

_____

_____

_____

THE DREAMKEEPER'S PRAYER FOCUS, PART 8

*May we work together in unity
to lift You up before all men, Lord Jesus,
so that they would be drawn to You
and receive eternal life.*

INCREASE YOUR POWER LEVEL— SOW SEEDS OF UNITY!

Insight for the Heart

If individual believers create unity within their local assembly, their power level goes up and their energy is not squandered needlessly. They can begin sowing seeds of unity within the entire community. Then, whole groups of churches begin to come together and realize that "they" are not the enemy! Great things begin to happen!

We get so mixed up as to who the enemy is. We have one enemy: Lucifer. He is the only enemy. There are other people who will harass and distract you, but they are not the enemy. *They may be tools of the enemy, but they are not the enemy.* They may shoot at you, but they are not enemy. They are being motivated by something somewhere. If you can get to the source, the root, and find out who or what is pushing their buttons and what is motivating them, then the problem can be solved. Check the foundation. (*God's Dream Team*, p. 90.)

Applications for Life

1. Can you think of situations in which *people* were mistakenly labeled as the enemy in a conflict within a local church? What fruit did these cases of mistaken identity produce?

2. Why is it important to accurately pinpoint the true enemy of the Church and God's people?

_____

_____

_____

_____

_____

_____

_____

_____

_____

_____

_____

_____

_____

_____

_____

_____

_____

_____

_____

_____

_____

_____

_____

_____

_____

THE DREAMKEEPER'S PRAYER FOCUS, PART 8

May we work together in unity
to lift You up before all men, Lord Jesus,
so that they would be drawn to You
and receive eternal life.

WE NEED TO PASTOR OUR CITIES SO REVIVAL CAN COME

Insight for the Heart

If we are going to reach our cities, we must change our mind-set. *It is time to stop pastoring our churches and start pastoring the cities in which we live.* As long as you just pastor your church, that's all you'll ever have. But if you can start pastoring your city, then revival will come to your city. It is time for the gatekeepers to take their places in the gates and to guard the source of influence over a city!

Much of what happened in Sodom and Gomorrah can be blamed on Lot—he didn't do what he had the authority to do. The Bible says, "Lot sat in the gate."[1] If you're a gatekeeper, that means you have a measure of control over what comes in and what goes out. You can say, "We want to keep this" or "We don't want this in our city." Lot allowed himself to be preempted by peer pressure or whatever else it was until he became acquiescent and allowed things to come into that city that he should have taken a stand against. (*God's Dream Team*, p. 90.)

Applications for Life

1. If you do not pastor a church, how can the truths in this reading be applied in your life?

2. In a sense, you are a gatekeeper with a measure of authority in every area of your life, whether it is in the home, on the job or at the local bowling alley. How can you begin to function as a spiritual gatekeeper?

Note
1. Gen. 19:1, *KJV*.

| THE DREAMKEEPER'S PRAYER FOCUS, PART 8 |

May we work together in unity
to lift You up before all men, Lord Jesus,
so that they would be drawn to You
and receive eternal life.

THINKING OF YOUR HOME IN KINGDOM TERMS

Insight for the Heart

Perhaps in troubled times, you have entertained the thought, *It is all I can do just to preserve my* own *household.* In the end, Lot even failed to do that. His two daughters were so corrupted that when they left Sodom and Gomorrah, they seduced their own father—and created two eternal enemies of Israel in their sons, Moab and Ammon. While Lot thought he was preserving his household, the powerful impact of the city had so corrupted his own house that he did not recognize it. We need to stop thinking locally and start thinking in terms of the whole city. It is simply part of HIS KINGDOM.

When you think in terms of HIS KINGDOM it will change the way you view things. (*God's Dream Team*, pp. 90, 91.)

Application for Life

1. What are some practical ways you can personally begin to think in terms of your whole city instead of merely thinking of your local church, your circle of friends or your family?

_____

_____

_____

_____

_____

_____

_____

_____

_____

_____

_____

_____

_____

_____

_____

_____

_____

_____

_____

_____

_____

_____

_____

_____

_____

_____

_____

_____

_____

_____

THE DREAMKEEPER'S PRAYER FOCUS, PART 8

*May we work together in unity
to lift You up before all men, Lord Jesus,
so that they would be drawn to You
and receive eternal life.*

TIME TO STAND TOGETHER AS THE CITY CHURCH

Insight for the Heart

There is a new movement coming—one in which ministerial and church relationships are not going to be with someone 300 miles away or with some church on the other side of the country. God is beginning to raise up "city churches" where your brothers and sisters are those with whom you stand guard in the gates of your city. If the gatekeepers take their places and stand strong together, then the Body of Christ can have an indelible impact on what comes into and gets put out of our cities. As long as we are content to guard only our little homes or our little church groups, our cities will be in trouble. We, the gatekeepers, must take our places. If you guard your gate but I don't guard mine, the city is still vulnerable. It's time for us to stand together! (*God's Dream Team*, p. 91.)

Applications for Life

1. In what ways can you help your brother at "First Church" down the road take his place as a gatekeeper (and vice versa)?

2. If God leads you to others who share the dream of answering God's prayer, are you willing to stand with them even though you will be misunderstood and distrusted at times? Are you willing to pay the price for true unity in the Body of Christ?

_____

_____

_____

_____

_____

_____

_____

_____

_____

_____

_____

_____

_____

_____

_____

_____

_____

_____

_____

_____

_____

_____

_____

_____

_____

_____

_____

_____

| THE DREAMKEEPER'S PRAYER FOCUS, PART 8 |

May we work together in unity
to lift You up before all men, Lord Jesus,
so that they would be drawn to You
and receive eternal life.

IF YOU WILL SERVE YOUR CITY, YOU WILL EARN THE RIGHT TO LEAD YOUR CITY

Insight for the Heart

If you will serve your city, you can lead your city—whether you lead in prayer or witnessing or pastoring. Without the fear of man you can face your city, serve among its gatekeepers and create unity that brings revival! (*God's Dream Team*, p. 92.)

Applications for Life

1. Are you willing to *serve* your city, even when its people and its leaders may not want or appreciate your sacrificial service? (Jesus already did it for *you*.)

2. Are you willing to serve even when your service may be mostly unseen and thankless—except in the eyes of God?

_____

_____

_____

_____

_____

_____

_____

_____

_____

_____

_____

_____

_____

_____

_____

_____

_____

_____

_____

_____

_____

_____

_____

_____

_____

_____

_____

_____

_____

THE DREAMKEEPER'S PRAYER FOCUS, PART 8

May we work together in unity
to lift You up before all men, Lord Jesus,
so that they would be drawn to You
and receive eternal life.

WHO ARE THE GATEKEEPERS FOR YOUR CITY?

Insight for the Heart

The obvious gatekeepers in your city include the pastors, intercessors and teachers in the spiritual realm and, in the secular realm, include the bankers, lawyers, professors, doctors, government officials, civic leaders and the captains of industry and business. However, you might be surprised to learn the identity of one of the less-than-obvious gatekeepers—you! The answer to the question of who is a gatekeeper is closely linked to the principle behind the question "Who is my neighbor?"[1]

Jesus worked for three long years to change the mind-sets of His religion-bound disciples. The battle for their minds reached its peak when Jesus confronted the disciples' entrenched racial prejudices and religious assumptions with the parable of the good Samaritan.[2]

I assume you already know the story, but have you noticed that Jesus set up His disciples by answering the "Who is my neighbor?" question using an example featuring a victim and two negligent gatekeepers *from their own cultural and religious comfort zone*? The Lord's hero—the compassionate person who invested time and money and risked personal reputation to help a fallen Jew—was a despised member of what the disciples thought was a second-class "denomination" and race. One of the most powerful statements in the New Testament is this: "You will know them by their fruits."[3]

Who is your neighbor? Anyone in need.

Who are the gatekeepers in your city? Anyone and everyone who has the power to exert spiritual influence in Christ's name—including you and every other true believer, regardless of the names and denominational titles on their church signs.

Notes
1. Luke 10:29.
2. See Luke 10:30-37.
3. Matt. 7:16. Jesus repeated this statement twice within the space of five verses! This indicates a divine emphasis that cannot be ignored. See Matthew 7:16-20 to capture the full impact of Jesus' statements.

Applications for Life

1. It is settled then: You are a gatekeeper in your city. What are you going to do now? Will you paint a sign damning all unbelievers to hell and position yourself in front of city hall? Or will you begin to seek God for ways to serve your city with Christlike love?

2. According to Jesus, how will the people of your city know you and recognize your true credentials as a gatekeeper?

THE DREAMKEEPER'S PRAYER FOCUS, PART 8

*May we work together in unity
to lift You up before all men, Lord Jesus,
so that they would be drawn to You
and receive eternal life.*

PART 4

THE
ENEMIES
OF UNITY

GOD WANTS TO HEAL THE PARAPLEGIC CHURCH

Insight for the Heart

According to Ephesians, Christ is the head of the Church and we are the body.[1] Think about this: How long has God struggled with a crippled Body? How long has He been troubled by cells wanting to disconnect from each other or refusing to connect in the first place?

A paralysis of purpose has invaded the Body of Christ; yet our Head still thinks with divine clarity. He wants His hand to move, but it will not obey. He bids His feet to walk, but they will not go. He sends signals for His tongue to speak, but it refuses to act. Can you believe it? This is a picture of the great mind of Christ—captured within the crippled body of a divisive Church. (*God's Dream Team*, pp. 102, 103.)

Applications for Life

1. Consider how frustrated you feel when you wake up in the morning and discover that somehow your leg or arm has gone to sleep and it won't respond or carry any weight. Do you think Jesus could say this about His earthly Body?

2. How do you respond to God's gentle impulses and directives? Are you sluggish and unresponsive or do you act instantly?

Note
1. See Eph. 4:15.

_____
_____
_____
_____
_____
_____
_____
_____
_____
_____
_____
_____
_____
_____
_____
_____
_____
_____
_____
_____
_____
_____
_____
_____
_____

THE DREAMKEEPER'S PRAYER FOCUS, PART 9

Oh God, I covenant with You.
Let us become one.
Command Your blessing upon us once again
as we dwell, serve, dream and worship You
together in blessed unity.

BE SURE TO TEND THE GARDEN OF YOUR MIND

Insight for the Heart

The enemies of unity take many forms, but very often they are clustered around their favorite fence-building materials of *gender, race, economic status* and *culture.*

All these bring with them certain human baggage that easily becomes fertile ground for the planting of vicious seeds of discord. We must constantly till and tend the gardens of our minds so that the weeds of disunity will never be allowed to bloom. When they do, they must be dealt with quickly. (*God's Dream Team*, pp. 103, 104.)

Applications for Life

1. Have you ever thought of your mind as a garden that must be tended? Do you think this is a valid analogy? Why or why not?

2. When discord has entered your mind and heart in the past, did you find that it was rooted in the "fence-building materials" described above? Explain.

_____

_____

_____

_____

_____

_____

_____

_____

_____

_____

_____

_____

_____

_____

_____

_____

_____

_____

_____

_____

THE DREAMKEEPER'S PRAYER FOCUS, PART 9

Oh God, I covenant with You.
Let us become one.
Command Your blessing upon us once again
as we dwell, serve, dream and worship You
together in blessed unity.

LACK OF COMPASSION PRODUCES SPIRITUAL BARRENNESS

Insight for the Heart

As far as I can tell, all of the miracles of Jesus recorded in the Bible were birthed out of compassion. Our lack of compassion is probably what produces barrenness in the Church. We need a rebirth of compassion that moves upon our hearts to share what we have with those who are lower on the economic scale. Godly compassion may well be one of the spiritual keys that will open to us the pure power of the miraculous. *Be as rich as you can be, but be as generous as you should be.* (*God's Dream Team*, p. 104.)

Applications for Life

1. Is compassion evident in the life and gatherings of your local church? Explain.

2. Is compassion evident in your own life each day? Give examples. If not, what will you do about it?

_____

_____

_____

_____

_____

_____

_____

_____

_____

┌───┐
THE DREAMKEEPER'S PRAYER FOCUS, PART 9
└───┘

Oh God, I covenant with You.
Let us become one.
Command Your blessing upon us once again
as we dwell, serve, dream and worship You
together in blessed unity.

CHURCHES OF A NEW BREED DRAW TOGETHER THE POOR AND THE PROSPEROUS

Insight for the Heart

There are huge gaps between the upper and lower classes in our society. Whether people come from secluded mansions hidden behind the gates of guarded communities or from one of the thousands of apartments clustered in the projects or from government-funded housing for the underprivileged, all socioeconomic groups should find a place of belonging in Christ.

There is a new breed of churches rising in which poverty can sit with prosperity without bitterness. And prosperity can sit with poverty without "betterness." Oh God, let it happen! (*God's Dream Team*, p. 105.)

Applications for Life

1. Can poverty sit with prosperity without bitterness in your local church's services? Why or why not?

2. Why is it healthy to have different classes of society gathered together in a local body of Christ?

_____

_____

_____

_____

_____

_____

THE DREAMKEEPER'S PRAYER FOCUS, PART 9

Oh God, I covenant with You.
Let us become one.
Command Your blessing upon us once again
as we dwell, serve, dream and worship You
together in blessed unity.

CULTURAL BARRIERS MUST DISAPPEAR UNDER THE BLOOD

Insight for the Heart

There are as many cultural differences in the Church as there are in society at large, and that is the way it should be! The human composition of the Church should closely mirror the composition of the communities it serves. At the same time, the Church should model the grace and mercy of God toward our differences. For instance, the liturgical church on the corner should openly appreciate and support the gifts and unorthodox methods of the street preacher who reaches those the liturgical church will never reach (and vice versa). Cultural characteristics are a blessing, but cultural barriers must disappear under the cleansing blood of Jesus, who openly mingled with prostitutes as well as prophets. It made no difference to Him; it should make no difference to us. To each his own: to all Christ and Him in us! (*God's Dream Team*, p. 106.)

Applications for Life

1. Are there cultural barriers in your local church or in your own life which separate you from other believers? What will you do about them?

2. Would you be comfortable eating in a local restaurant with the visiting prophet on one side of you and the prostitute who received Christ that night on the other side? Why or why not?

_____

_____

_____

_____

_____
_____
_____
_____
_____
_____
_____
_____
_____
_____
_____
_____
_____
_____
_____
_____
_____
_____
_____
_____
_____
_____

THE DREAMKEEPER'S PRAYER FOCUS, PART 9

Oh God, I covenant with You.
Let us become one.
Command Your blessing upon us once again
as we dwell, serve, dream and worship You
together in blessed unity.

Do You Know More Than You Can Explain?

Insight for the Heart

It always amazes me when I encounter people who have actually become *educated beyond their intelligence*. I am convinced that it is possible for us to get to a point where we know more than we can explain. When that happens, we must change our perspective and line up with Jesus. He knew all things, yet His teaching was so clear that little children understood what He said. This was no stuffy, intellectual religious leader who was too busy for the foolishness of children; they delighted to sit in His lap and He was delighted to accommodate them. (There is something in me that inherently mistrusts people whom children don't trust.) When we placard our walls with our academic degrees and lean on our own understanding and education, we tend to overlook the simplicity of the gospel. (*God's Dream Team*, pp. 106, 107.)

Applications for Life

1. Do you ever feel something inside you puff up when someone asks you a question about God or the Bible, something for which you feel you know the answer? Describe the situation.

2. How do you handle it? Do you relish that gloating feeling or dismiss it and answer the question simply and with humility?

_____

_____

_____

_____

_____

_____
_____
_____
_____
_____
_____
_____
_____
_____
_____
_____
_____
_____
_____
_____
_____
_____
_____
_____
_____
_____
_____

THE DREAMKEEPER'S PRAYER FOCUS, PART 9

Oh God, I covenant with You.
Let us become one.
Command Your blessing upon us once again
as we dwell, serve, dream and worship You
together in blessed unity.

RETURN TO THE SIMPLE BASICS OF WORSHIPING GOD AND MEETING NEEDS

Insight for the Heart

I have a mandate to call the Church to return to simple things—the basics. It doesn't matter who comes or who does not. This is not the time for lofty lectures on the science of hermeneutics on Sunday mornings (as preposterous as that might seem to some). I have no time to dabble in pragmatic epistemology—whatever that is. People are hurting. The wounded are waiting, and they come from every background, every educational level and every culture on the planet. (*God's Dream Team*, p. 107.)

Applications for Life

1. How many times has your life been deeply impacted by a lofty lecture on the science of hermeneutics? What *has* deeply impacted your life for good?

2. Do you believe that someone is hurting in virtually every meeting of the saints at your local church? Are those hurts and needs being met in any way? How can that change?

_____

_____

_____

_____

_____

_____

_____

_____

_____

_____

_____

_____

_____

_____

_____

_____

_____

_____

_____

_____

_____

_____

_____

_____

_____

_____

_____

THE DREAMKEEPER'S PRAYER FOCUS, PART 9

Oh God, I covenant with You.
Let us become one.
Command Your blessing upon us once again
as we dwell, serve, dream and worship You
together in blessed unity.

DON'T LET YOUR PAST STAND IN THE WAY OF YOUR FUTURE!

Insight for the Heart

Your past is a mystery to me as you read these words. Let me assure you, however, that both of us have long trails of history that color the way we view things in much the same way that rose-colored or dark-tinted sunglasses influence our vision on a sunny day. Your heritage—particularly the *pride* of heritage—can become one of the biggest barriers to unity in your relationships and in your local church. *Don't let your past stand in the way of your future,* whether your roots are in Mother Africa or Uncle Sam. Frankly, some of the traditions of our earthly fathers need to be exchanged for the traditions of the heavenly Father. (*God's Dream Team,* p. 108.)

Applications for Life

1. How does the problem with the pride of heritage compare with the dangers of the love of money? (Hint: Your heritage in and of itself isn't evil or wrong, just as money in and of itself isn't evil.)

2. Have you allowed your pride in some part of your heritage to hinder and limit your ability to relate to others and serve Jesus Christ? Is it really worth *that* much?

_____

_____

_____

_____

_____

_____

_____

_____

_____

_____

_____

_____

_____

_____

_____

_____

_____

_____

_____

_____

_____

_____

_____

_____

_____

_____

| THE DREAMKEEPER'S PRAYER FOCUS, PART 10 |

Dear Father,
I want one word to become my most passionate means
of communicating my love for You and Your kingdom.

When You seek my obedience, when You command my steps,
when You gently nudge me to step beyond my bounds
of comfort and ease,
I will say: "Yes, Lord. Not my will, but Yours."

I pray these things with thanksgiving in Jesus' name. Amen.

TRUE BIBLICAL UNITY PRODUCES REVIVAL AND A GREAT FLOOD OF NEW BELIEVERS

Insight for the Heart

True biblical unity will result in no-holds-barred, no-barriers-allowed revival and renewal in the Body of Christ. It will come bringing with it a great flood of new believers and will ultimately diminish the power of Satan in the world. No wonder the enemy would like to stop it before it ever begins, by sowing his favorite crops of disunity and discord. (*God's Dream Team*, p. 108.)

Applications for Life

1. Can you think of some of the things that would be moved aside and left behind in a no-holds-barred revival?

2. How can disunity and discord stop such a revival in its tracks?

_____

_____

_____

_____

_____

_____

_____

_____

_____

THE DREAMKEEPER'S PRAYER FOCUS, PART 10

Dear Father,
I want one word to become my most passionate means
of communicating my love for You and Your kingdom.

When You seek my obedience, when You command my steps,
when You gently nudge me to step beyond my bounds
of comfort and ease,
I will say: "Yes, Lord. Not my will, but Yours."

I pray these things with thanksgiving in Jesus' name. Amen.

NEWS FLASH: NOT ALL GROWTH IS OF GOD

Insight for the Heart

Paul wrote to Timothy,

> Be diligent to present yourself approved to God, a worker who does not need to be ashamed, rightly dividing the word of truth. But shun profane and idle babblings, for *they will increase* to more ungodliness. And their message will *spread like cancer.*[1]

Unregulated cell division is not growth; it's cancer. There are rogue cells among us that want growth at any cost. They will strive to take over the church body, disrupting the vital organs, stealing nourishment and ultimately bringing disunity to the body. All growth is not of God. In fact, *your* growth may not be Kingdom growth. Our corporate future is more important than our individual history. (*God's Dream Team*, p. 110.)

Applications for Life

1. Have you ever functioned as a rogue cell for a season? Have you been approached by a rogue cell who was sowing slander or rebellion in the local church body?

2. Carefully examine your life in Christ and ask yourself, *Is the growth and accomplishment in my life something God did or something I did apart from His blessing or command?* Then decide what you are going to do about it.

Note
1. 2 Tim. 2:15-17, emphasis mine.

_____
_____
_____
_____
_____
_____
_____
_____
_____
_____
_____
_____
_____
_____
_____
_____
_____
_____
_____
_____
_____
_____
_____

THE DREAMKEEPER'S PRAYER FOCUS, PART 10

Dear Father,
I want one word to become my most passionate means
of communicating my love for You and Your kingdom.

When You seek my obedience, when You command my steps,
when You gently nudge me to step beyond my bounds
of comfort and ease,
I will say: "Yes, Lord. Not my will, but Yours."

I pray these things with thanksgiving in Jesus' name. Amen.

WE ARE ONE TRIBE, WASHED IN THE BLOOD OF ONE LORD AND SAVIOR

Insight for the Heart

We live in a world where race relations are strained. In America, there has been a resurgence of the Ku Klux Klan's white-supremacist mentality. On other continents there are tribal wars. We should not, cannot, allow this to enter the Church. I find it interesting that when ministers of many different denominational and doctrinal backgrounds fellowship with one another, they often use the term "different tribes" to describe their diverse backgrounds. (*God's Dream Team*, pp. 110, 111.)

Applications for Life

1. Do you believe that a supremacist mentality of any kind is part of God's plan for the Church and for your life?

2. How does this kind of racist mentality match up with the multicultural ministry of Jesus and the apostle Paul? How does it compare to the way you live and think?

_____

_____

_____

_____

_____

_____

_____

_____

| THE DREAMKEEPER'S PRAYER FOCUS, PART 10 |

Dear Father,
I want one word to become my most passionate means
of communicating my love for You and Your kingdom.

When You seek my obedience, when You command my steps,
when You gently nudge me to step beyond my bounds
of comfort and ease,
I will say: "Yes, Lord. Not my will, but Yours."

I pray these things with thanksgiving in Jesus' name. Amen.

MAY THE COLOR LINE BE WASHED AWAY IN THE BLOODLINE!

Insight for the Heart

Unity is achieved through tolerance. The Bible allows us the privilege of tolerating someone with whom we differ—whether that difference is a simple difference of opinion, a different culture or a different income bracket. One of the journalists who recorded some of the Azusa Street revival stated, "The color line was washed away by the bloodline."[1] (*God's Dream Team*, p. 111.)

Application for Life

1. The world preaches tolerance, too; but the Church practices tolerance by focusing on our joint inheritance in Christ. He died for all, regardless of race, color, nationality or economic status. In what ways do you exercise tolerance with members of your local church?

Note
1. Source unknown.

_____

_____

_____

_____

_____

_____

_____

_____

_____

_____

_____

_____

_____

_____

_____

_____

| THE DREAMKEEPER'S PRAYER FOCUS, PART 10 |

Dear Father,
I want one word to become my most passionate means
of communicating my love for You and Your kingdom.

When You seek my obedience, when You command my steps,
when You gently nudge me to step beyond my bounds
of comfort and ease,
I will say: "Yes, Lord. Not my will, but Yours."

I pray these things with thanksgiving in Jesus' name. Amen.

BIBLICAL UNITY CAN BE DESTROYED BY SELFISHNESS

Insight for the Heart

Within the Body of Christ there will be differences—differences of opinion, differences of culture, differences of interpretation. However, we can have *unity in diversity* if we will learn to be as Paul and become "all things to all people."[1] Too often we cling to our own personal opinions and close-minded interpretations to the detriment and destruction of unity in the Body. *Biblical unity can be destroyed by selfishness; it can be created by self-less-ness.* God's approval is more important than our personal opinions. (*God's Dream Team*, p. 112.)

Applications for Life

1. Have you ever come to the point where one of your personal opinions or interpretations had to be discarded or kept private to preserve unity in your local church? If not, do you think you could discard an opinion or simply keep it to yourself to preserve unity?

2. What is the difference between true biblical unity centered on Christ and God's Word, and unanimity created through compromise of convictions and truth? (Yes, there *is* a difference.)

Note
1. 1 Cor. 9:22, *NRSV*.

_____

_____

_____

_____

_____
_____
_____
_____
_____
_____
_____
_____
_____
_____
_____
_____
_____
_____
_____
_____
_____

THE DREAMKEEPER'S PRAYER FOCUS, PART 10

Dear Father,
I want one word to become my most passionate means
of communicating my love for You and Your kingdom.

When You seek my obedience, when You command my steps,
when You gently nudge me to step beyond my bounds
of comfort and ease,
I will say: "Yes, Lord. Not my will, but Yours."

I pray these things with thanksgiving in Jesus' name. Amen.

ALLOW YOUR DIFFERENCES TO BE YOUR STRENGTHS IN UNITY

Insight for the Heart

Paul spoke of men being called to be prophets and pastors and teachers.[1] In some ways this is a built-in invitation to conflict. A pastor will view things from a pastor's perspective and with a pastor's heart. A teacher will want to instruct and educate. A prophet will want to focus not on what is but what can be. However, biblical unity results when we agree to allow our differences to be our strengths and become a consolidated, amalgamated, but not uniform Body of Christ. Racial reconciliation should exactly model this, with our differences becoming our strengths. Color is skin deep; but culture and heritage deepen the gap. His blood will bridge that chasm. "There is neither Jew nor Greek, there is neither slave nor free, there is neither male nor female; for you are all one in Christ Jesus."[2] (*God's Dream Team*, pp. 113, 114.)

Applications for Life

1. Can you see how the different perspectives and strengths of the five ministry gifts mentioned in Ephesians 4—apostles, prophets, evangelists, pastors and teachers—could lead to different ways of seeing and doing things? Did God make a mistake? Obviously not. How can these differences produce blessing in the Church?

2. If God didn't make a mistake in making all of *us* different, then how can our differences produce blessing in the Church and to the lost?

Notes
1. See Eph. 4:11.
2. Gal. 3:28.

_____

_____

_____

_____

_____

_____

_____

_____

_____

_____

_____

_____

_____

_____

_____

_____

_____

| THE DREAMKEEPER'S PRAYER FOCUS, PART 10 |

Dear Father,
I want one word to become my most passionate means
of communicating my love for You and Your kingdom.

When You seek my obedience, when You command my steps,
when You gently nudge me to step beyond my bounds
of comfort and ease,
I will say: "Yes, Lord. Not my will, but Yours."

I pray these things with thanksgiving in Jesus' name. Amen.

PART 5

ANSWERING CHRIST'S PRAYER

by Francis Frangipane

Adapted from "Becoming the Answer to Christ's Prayer,"
which appeared in In Christ's Image, *an Internet*
publication of Arrow Publications, at www.frangipane.org.
Used by permission.

If you look closely at the 12 disciples of the Lamb, you will see that God got a mixed lot with those men. Matthew was a former "IRS agent." James and John were former "fundamentalists" who abandoned meaningful employment with their father to church-hop to an itinerant lifestyle in the Jesus Movement. Two of the disciples, Simon the Zealot and Judas Iscariot, were extreme nationalists, the social equivalent of modern right-wing militiamen.

Most of the others were simple, uneducated blue-collar workers. The educated religious elite of that day called them mere fishermen, the ignorant and unlearned. Jesus called them His *own.*

These aren't the most likely candidates to upend the status quo and establish a new Kingdom on earth, but they were the people God chose. No wonder Jesus was praying for them to become one! He invested three long years in these widely diverse men and the company of women who supported His ministry.[1] He put up with seemingly endless squabbles over who was "first" in the group, who would sit at His right hand in heaven (and perhaps on earth) and how the money in the common purse would be handled. In other words, He knows *exactly* what goes on in the average church body today because He experienced it personally.

SATAN HATES CHRISTIAN UNITY

Christ's disciples were divided along many lines. How did Jesus react to their divisions and differences? We know that He did not sanction their divisions, nor did He pretend they did not exist. Jesus refused to lower His expectations for unity just to match the level of carnality demonstrated by His disciples. Instead He prayed for their standards to be raised to the oneness of the Godhead! He is doing the same for us today.

The Spirit of Christ who dwells within us is pleading for our unity. How can we be so deaf to His desires, so cold toward His passions? How can we say we love Him and not keep His commandments or embrace His vision for us?

SATAN MAKES UNIMPORTANT THINGS ALL-IMPORTANT TO SELF-IMPORTANT MEN

Meanwhile, Satan the adversary is doing everything he can to entice us to take our focus off Jesus. The devil manipulates our natural and cultural distinctions and magnifies them into compelling reasons to divide from other born-again Christians. He works tirelessly to make things that are unimportant to God all-important to self-important men.

Frankly, the petty issues that divide born-again Christians are not really *our* conflicts. Truth is true, with or without our help or agreement.

God is fully God, whether we all describe and worship Him in the same way or not. He is well able to correct error, reprove wrongs, redirect misdirected emphases and reform errant theology. His problem is changing our foolish actions without violating our free wills.

Underlying all the division in the Body of Christ is a larger cosmic conflict between Satan and the Lord Jesus. The devil is *not* the Lord's equal; he is only a created being. He is powerless to directly touch the Lord who defeated him and stripped him of his power long ago. Instead, Satan devotes his efforts toward exploiting *our* divisions to grieve the Holy Spirit and prolong the Lord's wait for the answer to His most passionate prayer.

We must see that when we continue in our carnal divisions and bickering ways, we are actually reinforcing the deceptions of the devil himself—no matter how much we claim to be defending the truth.

I am amazed and dismayed when I see how many born-again Christians have allowed Satan to convince them that unity with other believers is evil! It is difficult to find a more dangerous false doctrine that is so widespread and so accepted in the Body of Christ. It is absolutely contrary to the heart and teachings of Christ—yet division has become an unspoken *tradition* within the Church!

THEY LOVE GOD, BUT THEY HAVE A PROBLEM WITH SOME OF HIS PEOPLE

Entire families of churches actually take pride in their antagonistic differences and elaborate efforts to separate themselves from other churches. I'll never forget a conversation I had recently with a pastor who genuinely loves God but has a problem loving His people if they differ from him.

"Show me in the Bible!" the pastor challenged me. "Show me where God says our different churches are supposed to be united."

I tried to restrain myself but it wasn't easy. I didn't want to overwhelm him with the hundreds of Scriptures that call us to unity with other born-again Christians.

I had heard his complaint before. According to the theology held by my new acquaintance, for him to say "Okay, I'll unite in prayer with other pastors" was tantamount to saying "Yes, I'll join the One World Church and follow the Antichrist." In his mind, any unity with other churches was blatantly false because it would require him to close his eyes to "doctrinal error" and be swallowed up in the "great falling away."

I took a breath and prayed silently for the wisdom and gentleness of Christ. Long ago I realized that when people study the Bible, many times they will only read what they already believe instead of believing what they read.

Should I take our discussion to the book of Romans where Paul describes a variety of ways to bring Jewish and Gentile Christians into unity?[2] Would it be better to mention the epistles of First and Second Corinthians, where Paul rebukes Christians for their divisions while calling the Church to their highest diversity and harmony?[3]

I was having a difficult time making up my mind because so much of the New Testament is devoted to the subject of unity. Since I didn't have much time, I went right to John 17, where Jesus not only talks about the unity of Christians but also reveals the deepest longing of His heart as He fervently prays and pleads for unity. Surely the Lord's passionate prayer for unity would soften this doctrine-hardened heart.

"Do you think the Scripture passage is true which claims that 'Jesus Christ is the same yesterday, today, and forever'?" I asked.[4] My pastor friend quickly nodded his head affirmatively. "Would it be safe to imagine that since Jesus 'ever lives to make intercession'[5] for the Church, and that He always prays according to the will of His Father, that He would be praying for the same things today that He asked for in the first century?" Again, he agreed. The foundation of agreement was laid. At that point I asked my new friend to turn to the Gospel of John.

JOHN 17 REVEALS THE HEART OF GOD

Anyone who truly studies Jesus' prayer in John 17 will, in my opinion, step right into His heart. That Bible chapter is nothing less than 26 verses of intimate communication between God the Father and God the Son. It is as if God permitted us to eavesdrop on His holy counsel for a brief moment in eternity. In that moment, we see how Jesus views people who are united as His followers while still clinging to the divisions caused by their own fears, ambitions and clashing worldviews. His disciples represent a microcosm, a miniature view, of the many-membered Body in contrast and dynamic tension.

We, like the Lord's first disciples, represent a wide disparity of doctrinal and social origins, and we have been known to argue about our positions of power or authority just as forcefully and foolishly as they did. We are all frequently subject to carnal ideas and hidden agendas, and we, like the disciples before us, demonstrate much of the time that we don't have the slightest idea of what Jesus meant when He taught the Word.

My minister friend was correct, of course, when he said we shouldn't unite with every so-called Christian or church organization. Sadly, there *are* many false Christians in the world, and Satan still likes to masquerade among men as an angel of light. Yet the chief question is not whether we will be led astray and become false. Our greatest challenge today is to humbly repent of the unbiblical divisions that divide born-again Christians and finally become truly one as Jesus and the Father are one!

THE SOURCE OF TRUE UNITY

How can we build unity God's way? We've tried everything we know and we've failed miserably. Perhaps we should look at the three dynamics, or fundamental truths, that Jesus gave us in His intimate conversation with the Father in John 17. The Lord said He would lead His Church into the same profound state of unity He enjoys with His Father in heaven. That state of oneness can only be accessed by correctly relating to God's *name*, His *Word* and His *glory*.

The first dynamic truth of God-ordained unity is found in John 17:11 (*NASB*): "Holy Father, keep them *in Thy name*, the name which Thou hast given Me, that they may be one, even as We are" (emphasis mine). God calls us into unity with everyone who has called upon the name of the Lord. This is a wide umbrella. Notice that the unity Jesus is asking for in this passage is not based on common interpretation of doctrinal positions; it is based on the power of God's name and our common need of His help.

The fact is that we are already united under the redemptive power of Christ's name. This redemption is not something we can earn or attain. It is a finished, completed work that we must acknowledge and accept from God alone.

We must face the fact that when we bow our knees before Him and position ourselves at the foot of His cross, we are all brought to the same level and the same divine grace. When we turn our eyes away from judging and comparing one another to gaze upon His glorious face, we are one. The name of Jesus has given us a positional oneness, or unity, before the Cross.

Secondly, the *words* of Jesus can bring us into functional oneness. There is only one authority and one voice qualified to define this term. Again we turn to the prayer of Jesus:

I do not ask in behalf of these alone, but for those also who believe in Me *through their word*; that they may all be one; even as Thou, Father, art in Me, and I in Thee, that they also may be in Us; that the world may believe that Thou didst send Me.[6]

When Jesus prayed for unity in His church, He never expected that unity to flow from man's innate ability to organize himself around projects or ideals.

UNITY CAUSES THE WORLD TO BELIEVE

When Jesus prayed "for those also who believe in Me through their word," He was confirming our responsibility to pass on to others the Word He has given us so they, too, can believe. A function of visible unity among Christians is that it causes the world—the non-Christian population—to believe that God sent Jesus into the world to save mankind. This is the very heart of the Great Commission, which Jesus gave to the Church before He ascended into heaven.[7]

Christ's life, as embodied in both His redemptive mission and His teaching, is the foundational reality of Christianity. His sacrifice atones for our past; His Word establishes and creates our future. It is here that true oneness and Christian discipleship emerge.

God has given us His name and His words to create and establish oneness in the Church. Yet the last stage of unity is the highest and most wonderful.

The third dynamic truth or fundamental for building unity in the Body is also revealed in Jesus' prayer:

And *the glory* which Thou hast given Me I have given to them; that they may be one, just as We are one; I in them, and Thou in Me, that they may be perfected in unity, that the world may know that Thou didst send Me, and didst love them, even as Thou didst love Me.[8]

This is the height and goal of true Christianity—the revelation of Jesus Christ through His Church. We receive *provisional oneness* through His name, *functional oneness* created and maintained through Christ's words, and the awe of a *living oneness* produced by Christ's indwelling glory.

This is not something that will only happen in the sweet by and by. Jesus was praying about something that is so explicitly here and now that it will cause the unsaved world to believe.

That is a survey of what Jesus prayed to His Father. A survey of what the Church is really like today is sadly different from this picture. So how do we get from here to there?

WE CAN ANSWER HIS PRAYER

Like so many things in the kingdom of God, Jesus' great dream can be and *must be* answered by one act at a time, one decision at a time. I desperately want to give something back to my wonderful Savior, and I think it is reasonable to believe you feel as I do.

Jesus is the Father's great answer for all of my prayers. When I ask God for guidance, I receive Jesus as my Great Shepherd. When I am sick, I receive Jesus as my Healer, for by His stripes I was healed. When I confess to God that I am perplexed, I am reminded that Jesus is my Teacher. However, there is something we can give back to Him. As Tommy Tenney has said, "We can be the answer to His prayer for unity."

Each time we choose to pray for others rather than criticize them, we have become part of the answer to Jesus' prayer. Every time we turn and forgive a brother who has hurt us, we become a welcome answer to the Master's deepest longing. When we unite with other churches in love, in prayer, in good deeds and humble, joyful service, we bring pleasure to His heart and renewed hope that His answer is near.

Think of it: We may be small and otherwise ordinary in comparison to other people or compared to the grand scale of God's vision. Yet we, and only we, can be the answer to the fervent prayer of God's Son: "Father, make them one."

Notes
1. All three Synoptic Gospels describe this group of women who supported Jesus and the disciples financially and followed them whenever they were ministering near Galilee (see Matt. 27:55,56; Mark 15:40,41; Luke 8:2,3; 23:55; 24:10,22).
2. See Rom. 3:22,23,29; 4:16,17; 5:16-19; 6:5; 12; 14; 16.
3. See 1 Cor. 1:10-13; 3:1-4, 21-23; 12—14; 2 Cor. 12:20,21.
4. Heb. 13:8.
5. See Rom. 8:27; Heb. 7:25.
6. John 17:20,21, *NASB*, emphasis mine.
7. See Matt. 28:20.
8. John 17:22,23, *NASB*, emphasis mine.

A PREMIUM ON UNITY

Duane Elmer writes in his book *Cross-Cultural Conflict*:

> The Western world does not place a high premium on unity. Wherever individualism reigns supreme, community is easily sacrificed for personal preferences. Although I enjoy the luxuries of individualism, I cannot help but feel it has also brought a certain impoverishment. Too quickly we splinter churches, friendships, families and groups rather than struggle for ways to bridge differences, reconnect, forgive, reconcile and heal.
>
> The dubious luxury of disposable relationships has a dark side, a serious dark side. Failures in individual and community relationships cast aspersions on God's reputation. These fractures are noticed by the unbelieving world. If God cannot keep His own people from becoming adversaries, why should a reflective onlooker consider becoming a Christian? A fractured body is dysfunctional. The ability to respect human and cultural differences and not let them disrupt harmony is powerful testimony to the love and power of God.[1]

According to the Scriptures in John 17, our greatest strength as the Body of Christ lies in the fact that although we are different individuals, we are one in Him. Western culture and many churches in the Western hemisphere view "community unity" with lingering suspicion and weak interest; but it is actually *proof* of God's presence among us, and it can become our greatest strength.

Unity has a high cost, but its value is almost beyond calculation in the economy and purposes of God. The sacrifice of our own autonomy to His sovereignty would almost seem easier if it required the sacrifice of an animal rather than the sacrifice of an agenda—especially if it were *somebody else's* lamb. It becomes even more difficult when it is *our* lamb or our agenda.

In a very real sense, God sacrificed His beloved Lamb to bring divine unity to the earth. Now the Lamb of God is waiting for you and me to follow His lead and crawl up on the altar of obedience and death to self to become the fulfillment of God's greatest dream.

I hear the plea of God's heart echoed in the entreaty of the book of Romans:

> I beseech you therefore, brethren, by the mercies of God, that you *present your bodies a living sacrifice*, holy, acceptable to God, which is your reasonable service.[2]

Jesus has already etched the will of God into the gospel record with the acid-hot tears and bloody intercession of His passion in the garden of Gethsemane. Now it's our turn. It is up to you and me to join together and become the living answer to His most fervent prayer.

Your brother and partner in the pursuit of His dream,

Tommy Tenney

Notes

1. Duane Elmer, *Cross-Cultural Conflict: Building Relationships For Effective Ministry* (Downers Grove, IL: InterVarsity Press, 1993), n.p.
2. Rom. 12:1, emphasis mine.

THE DREAMKEEPER'S PRAYER

The Dreamkeeper's Prayer is adapted from my book *God's Dream Team* (pp. 144, 145). You have already prayed through each of the 10 segments of this prayer during your time of study and biblical meditation upon God's Word. As the final step toward answering God's most passionate prayer, pray this prayer to Him once again and commit yourself to become a Dreamkeeper.

Lord, we long to answer Your prayer for unity
so that the world will know You are the Son of God
and that You have come from the Father.
Yet I know the "we" must begin with me.

I want to make You Lord of my life
and not merely call You Lord.
Holy Spirit, I ask You to convict and perfect me
so that I can accomplish what the Father has called me to do.

Grant me, and grant us, the grace to walk in humility,
considering others better than ourselves.
May we look after the interests of others
as carefully as we look after our own.
Above all, may my attitude be the same as Yours—
that of a humble servant.

Father, forgive me for my selfish motives and my envy of others.
Lord Jesus, let my heart be broken like Your heart,
and may I humble myself to serve others
as faithfully as You served us in Your life, death and resurrection;
let there be no division between me and my brethren.

I pray that my kingdom would go so that Your kingdom may come.
May my will be broken so that Your will may be done
on earth as it is in heaven.

Lord, cause me to be single-minded
and sure of Your calling upon my life.
May unity of heart and mind prevail in my home,
in my community of friends and family,
in my local church and in the Church around the world
as we focus upon You, our risen Lord, Master, King and Savior.

Break down the barriers that separate us,
and bind Your people together again in Your love.
Raise up those among us who have fallen.
Cause Your compassion to stir our hearts
and impregnate us with Your purposes.
May our chief loyalty be to You and to everyone
who shares our common bloodline in the Lamb who was slain.

May we work together in unity to lift You up before all men, Lord Jesus,
so that they would be drawn to You and receive eternal life.

Oh God, I covenant with You.
Let us become one.
Command Your blessing upon us once again
as we dwell, serve, dream and worship You
together in blessed unity.

Dear Father,
I want one word to become my most passionate means
of communicating my love for You and Your kingdom.

When You seek my obedience, when You command my steps,
when You gently nudge me to step beyond my bounds of comfort and ease,
I will say: "Yes, Lord. Not my will, but Yours."

I pray these things with thanksgiving in Jesus' name. Amen.

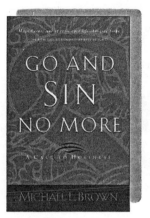

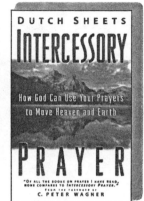

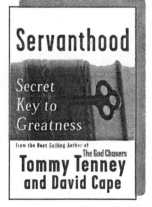
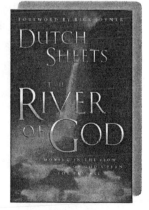

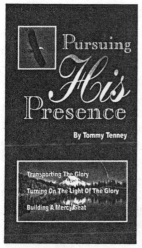

PURSUING HIS PRESENCE
(audiotape album) $20 plus $3 S&H

Tape 1 - Transporting the Glory: The only thing that can carry "the ark" (the glory of God) is sanctification, the developing of godly character. Also learn about "divine radiation zones" and hear an exciting testimony about a man's crushed hand that was miraculously healed, the repercussions of which affected his entire town!

Tape 2 - Turning On the Light of the Glory: This best-selling tape has literally gone around the world. Tommy deals with turning on the light of the glory and presence of God, and he walks us through the necessary process and ingredients to potentially unleash what His Body has always dreamed of—God dwelling in the Church to such a measure that there comes a great visitation of His presence to bring revival in the land.

Tape 3 - Building a Mercy Seat: If we build the mercy seat—in the spiritual sense—according to the pattern that God gave to Moses, the same thing will happen as occurred when the original was built. The presence of God came and dwelt between the outstretched wings of the worshiping cherubim. In worshiping, we create an appropriate environment in which the presence of God can dwell, which was the whole focus of the Old Testament tabernacle.

FANNING THE FLAMES
(audiotape album) $20 plus $3 S&H

Tape 1 - The Application of the Blood and the Ark of the Covenant: Most of the churches in America today dwell in an outer-court experience. God said He would dwell in the mercy seat. Jesus' death and sacrifice paralleled the sacrifice of the high priest who entered behind the veil to make atonement with the blood of animals. Jesus made atonement with His own blood, once for all, and the veil in the temple was rent from top to bottom.

Tape 2 - A Tale of Two Cities—Nazareth & Ninevah: In this challenging message, Tommy contrasts Nazareth with Ninevah. Jesus spent more time in Nazareth than any other city, yet there was great resistance to the works of God there. A haughty spirit, arrogance, and unbelief are not fertile ground for the Lord to move. In contrast, consider the characteristics of the people of Ninevah.

Tape 3 - The "I" Factor: Examine the difference between *ikabod* and *kabod* ("glory"). The arm of flesh cannot achieve what needs to be done. God doesn't need us; we need Him. Our churches have been filled with noise, but devoid of worship. Real worship only comes from those who are willing to stand in the gap. Let the axe be laid to the root of the tree when it comes to religious spirits.

KEYS TO LIVING THE REVIVED LIFE
(audiotape album) $20 plus $3 S&H

Tape 1 - Fear Not: Fear is faith in reverse. Whatever faith accomplishes by progress, fear accomplishes by regression. The principles that Tommy reveals teach us that to have no fear is to have faith, and that perfect love casts out fear, so we establish the trust of a child in our loving Father. The Scriptures are replete with examples of heavenly messengers beginning their message with these two significant words, "Fear not." Obviously, it is a message from heaven for earth.

Tape 2 - Hanging In There: Have you ever been tempted to give up, quit, and throw in the towel? This message is a word of encouragement for you. Everybody has a place and a position in the Kingdom of God. Any of us can be as great as the most anointed teachers, pastors, and gifted men and women, because of one extremely important criterion for being a hero that often goes overlooked. Jeannie Tenney joins her husband and sings an inspiring chorus, "I'm going through."

Tape 3 - Fire of God: Fire purges the sewer of our souls and destroys the hidden things that would cause disease. Fire perfects our praise. How does a church living, for the most part, powerless, in defeat and shackled by shame, become free and walk in victory? Learn the way out of a repetitive cycle of seasonal times of failure. When the church becomes a place where people can expose their withered crippledness, healing will take place.

DYNAMIC CHRISTIAN LIVING
(audiotape album), $20 plus $3 S&H

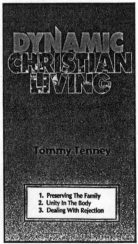

Tape 1 - Preserving the Family: This manifesto on the unsurpassed importance of preserving the integrity of the family unit highlights God's desire to heal the wounds of dysfunctional families, from the inside out.

Tape 2 - Unity in the Body: Despite the abuse of the term *unity*, godly unity in truth is a priority on our Father's heart. Tommy examines four levels of unity that must be respected and achieved before we will see the true unity that is so needed in the Body.

Tape 3 - Dealing With Rejection: No one has known continual rejection as much as Jesus did. As followers of Jesus, we know we will be despised and rejected. Here is concrete help in dealing victoriously with rejection and the life-sapping emotions that can result.